Living in Hostile Territory by the Grace of God

Living in Hostile Territory by the Grace of God

1 Peter

This inductive Bible study is designed for individual, small group, or classroom use. A leader's guide with full lesson plans and the answers to the Bible study questions is available from Regular Baptist Press. Order RBP0031 online at www.regularbaptistpress.org, e-mail orders@rbpstore.org, call toll-free 1-800-727-4440, or contact your distributor.

REGULAR BAPTIST PRESS
1300 North Meacham Road
Schaumburg, Illinois 60173-4806

The Doctrinal Basis of Our Curriculum

A more detailed statement with references is available upon request.

- The verbal, plenary inspiration of the Scriptures
- Only one true God
- The Trinity of the Godhead
- The Holy Spirit and His ministry
- The personality of Satan
- The Genesis account of creation
- Original sin and the fall of man
- The virgin birth of Christ
- Salvation through faith in the shed blood of Christ
- The bodily resurrection and priesthood of Christ
- Grace and the new birth
- Justification by faith
- Sanctification of the believer

- The security of the believer
- The church
- The ordinances of the local church: baptism by immersion and the Lord's Supper
- Biblical separation— ecclesiastical and personal
- Obedience to civil government
- The place of Israel
- The pretribulation rapture of the church
- The premillennial return of Christ
- The millennial reign of Christ
- Eternal glory in Heaven for the righteous
- Eternal torment in Hell for the wicked

LIVING IN HOSTILE TERRITORY BY THE GRACE OF GOD: 1 PETER
Adult Bible Study Book
Vol. 59, No. 1
© 2010
Regular Baptist Press • Schaumburg, Illinois
www.regularbaptistpress.org • 1-800-727-4440
Printed in U.S.A.
All rights reserved
RBP0034 • ISBN: 978-1-60776-330-7

Contents

Preface

Does your life seem like a battlefield? Do trials and suffering threaten to undo you? Do you feel like you are living in hostile territory? You are not alone. Trials and suffering are part of the Christian life. In fact, Peter wrote a letter to a group of believers telling them that they should not think of their trials, suffering, and persecution as strange. Peter's letter, 1 Peter, is the focus of this Bible study.

If see your struggles as cause for despair and doubt, then you need a fresh outlook. First Peter will help you change your perspective on the difficulties of life. You will begin to see them as opportunities for growth and as avenues of God's blessings. You will learn that joy and satisfaction are possible in the midst of your struggles. And you will realize both God's power and comfort to help you through each day.

God doesn't offer an escape hatch from suffering. So if that is what you are looking for, then you won't be helped by this study. What God does offer by His grace is so much better than an escape hatch. Learn more about what is available to you as you study about *Living in Hostile Territory by the Grace of God*.

Lesson 1

Comeback

God desires that we come back from spiritual failure in our lives.

1 Peter 1:1, 2

"And Jesus, walking by the sea of Galilee, saw two brethren, Simon called Peter, and Andrew his brother, casting a net into the sea: for they were fishers. And he saith unto them, Follow me, and I will make you fishers of men" (Matthew 4:18, 19).

He was a maverick—one of those independent individuals who do not go along with their commanders. When he found about forty of the enemy, he thought their village would be easy pickings. In the arrogant, impulsive manner that had served him well in past engagements, he did not bother to gather intelligence about the terrain or the number of enemy soldiers in the camp. He attacked, and after a two-day battle, he and his men were defeated in one of the most famous failures in American history. The battle that wiped out his regiment is known today as the Battle of the Little Bighorn or as Custer's Last Stand. That summer, George Armstrong Custer was an epic failure in his strategy, his choices, and his behavior.

Getting Started

1. Describe a time when you miserably failed at a new venture.

9

2. How did you respond?

3. Did you eventually become successful in your venture? If so, what made the difference?

Peter was an epic failure spiritually, but Jesus did not let him give up. He challenged him and helped him to become an important part in God's ministry in the early church.

Searching the Scriptures

Just an 'Ignorant' Fisherman

Peter came from the town of Bethsaida (John 1:44). His father was Jona (or John; John 1:42), and he had at least one brother, Andrew (Matthew 4:18). Peter also had a wife (Matthew 8:14), although there is no record of her name or if they had children.

Peter was a fisherman by trade, a job he did with his brother (Matthew 4:18). Fishermen weren't known for their intelligence, though they knew how to work patiently and persistently.

4. Based on Peter's background, do you think you would have identified him as a person likely to succeed in ministry? Explain.

5. How would persistence and patience help Peter in ministry?

6. Read Acts 4:13. What made the ultimate difference for Peter as he ministered for the Lord?

Like a Rock

At the time of Peter's conversion, Christ gave him a new name. John 1:42 states, "Thou art Simon the son of Jona: thou shalt be called Cephas, which is by interpretation, A stone." His name by birth was Simon, "God has heard." Then Christ gave him the Aramaic name Cephas, which means a small stone or rock. The Greek equivalent is *petros*, from which we derive the name Peter.

This new name would show something about Christ's goal for Peter's character, that Peter would be bold and strong like a rock.

7. Read Luke 22:31–34. What three words do you think Peter would use to describe himself at this point in his life?

8. Do you think he would use the words "bold" and "strong" to describe himself? Explain.

Tested and Failed

Peter's denial of Christ probably marked the lowest point of his life. When Christ announced that someone would betray Him, Peter fervently declared that he would never do that. In response, the Lord predicted that Peter would deny Him three times before the rooster would crow in the morning.

Sadly, like all true prophecy, this came to pass. Peter denied Christ three times. He even swore that his lie was the truth. When all of this happened, Jesus simply looked at Peter. What a look that must have been. Peter, remembering Jesus' words, wept bitterly in repentance.

9. Read Luke 22:54–62. What three words would you use to describe Peter at this point in his life?

10. Do you think he would use the words "bold" and "strong" to describe himself? Explain.

Recommissioned

Peter's first commission came with the Lord's call: "Follow me, and I will make you fishers of men" (Matthew 4:19). He had been a fisher of fish, taking that which was alive from its natural habitat and bringing it into the realm of death. Christ called him to fish for people, taking those who were dead and bringing them into the realm of life in Christ. Jesus commissioned Peter to be a disciple or follower. He later would be chosen as an apostle.

Peter had a profitable three-year course under the Master Teacher, but at the end he experienced failure and finally went back to his fishing (John 21:3). It was at the seashore of Galilee that the Lord recommissioned him (vv. 15–22).

Before Peter could fulfill the Lord's design for his life, he needed restoration. For this reason the Lord probed his heart.

11. Read John 21:15. What heart-probing question did the Lord ask Peter?

Peter had once boasted that, in spite of the failures of others, he would never deny his Lord. After Peter's failure, the Lord knew that the old self-confidence was gone, and He encouraged Peter by entrusting to him an important ministry: "Feed my lambs." Two more times the Lord placed His finger on the tender spot in Peter's life, and two more times He expressed His confidence in Peter by commissioning him, "Feed my sheep." Peter still had to learn the lesson of complete obedience and singleness of purpose: "Follow thou me." He still needed to experience the enabling of Pentecost, but he was becoming a great apostle.

12. How do you think Peter was affected when Jesus confidently commissioned him to "feed His sheep"?

Peter needed to be challenged and commissioned again by Jesus. But going to our Savior is not always our first reaction when we fail Him.

13. How do believers sometimes respond when they fail the Lord?

An Apostle

Christ chose twelve of His disciples to be specially "sent ones," or apostles. One of them was Peter, who identified himself as an apostle in the very first verse of his letters. Peter was part of that inner circle of disciples, along with James and John, who were privileged to be with Christ on special occasions.

The Gospel accounts end soon after Peter's dismal spiritual failure and Christ's restoration of him. The book of Acts shows Peter as an enthusiastic, energetic worker for God: Peter served as chairman at the election of a replacement for Judas (Acts 1:15). He delivered the great sermon on the Day of Pentecost (2:14–40). He acted as the explainer (apologist) for the new faith (3:12–26; 4:8–12). He was the moderator in resolving the Ananias-Sapphira problem (5:1–11). He brought the message of salvation to Gentiles (10:34–48). He had the gospel to the circumcision (Jews) committed to him (Galatians 2:7). And, finally, he wrote the Biblical books that bear his name.

14. Based on Peter's life, how would you respond to the notion that God has no use for people who fail Him?

The First Letter

Peter wrote his first epistle from Babylon (1 Peter 5:13), but there is some question about the location of this "Babylon." Was this the literal city of Babylon, in the area now known as Iraq? Or was this a symbolic reference to Rome (as in Revelation 17)? Bible-believing, honest scholars stand on both sides of this question. The usual reading of this passage seems to indicate that he referred to the literal Babylon, since nothing hints that the name should be interpreted figuratively.

Peter probably wrote this epistle sometime around AD 63. This is determined from the fact that Nero's large-scale persecution of the church came in AD 64, and it seems that the people whom Peter was addressing were beginning to face, but had not fully encountered, that persecution for their faith.

Two persons are mentioned along with Peter in 1 Peter 5:12 and 13. Silvanus (Silas) was probably the messenger who carried the epistle and was perhaps the one who actually wrote down the words that Peter gave as directed by the Holy Spirit. Mark, probably the spiritual son of Peter, sent along his greetings as well, since he was near where Peter was living.

The Recipients

Peter spoke of his readers as "strangers scattered" throughout the five provinces of Pontus, Galatia, Cappadocia, Asia, and Bithynia. These areas today form most of Turkey.

"Strangers" indicates that they were aliens or temporary residents in the land. Peter was describing Jewish believers who had settled among non-Jewish people.

"Scattered" speaks of Jews living outside Palestine. They may have been in the five provinces by choice because of business opportunities, or they may have been scattered by reason of the persecutions following Pentecost. Jews from some of the very provinces Peter listed had gathered at Jerusalem when Peter preached his sermon and three thousand received his word and were baptized (Acts 2:9–11).

Three Facets of Redemption

15. Read 1 Peter 1:2. What was the readers' spiritual position?

From the human perspective we are well aware that the unsaved must receive Christ and believe on Him to be saved. Peter discussed salvation from the divine perspective and listed three facets of personal redemption.

The first facet is the act of God the Father, Who in a deliberative judgment (foreknowledge) chooses us from before the foundation of the world. Our election of God is demonstrated when we come to Jesus Christ in simple faith, for "all that the Father giveth me shall come to me; and him that cometh to me I will in no wise cast out" (John 6:37).

The second facet is the work of the Holy Spirit—"sanctification of the Spirit." The Holy Spirit takes the one chosen of God and sets him or her apart for conviction of unbelief, repentance toward God, and faith in Jesus Christ. The Holy Spirit uses the Word of God to bring us to faith in Christ.

The third facet is the justification and cleansing, which became ours through the blood of Jesus Christ.

Victory

16. Read 1 Peter 1:7. What is the purpose for Peter's letter, as found in this verse?

Woven throughout this book are several references to suffering and persecution (1:6, 7; 2:19–25; 3:16, 17; 4:12–19). The believers to whom Peter was writing were beginning to face actual persecution for their faith. Their persecution came because they lived out their faith in a hostile, pagan society. The persecution included slander, violent riots, and social rejection. Peter wrote to help the believers correctly handle their persecution and trials.

17. What does the impure gold symbolize in the key verse, 1 Peter 1:7?

18. What does the fire symbolize?

19. To what does the pure gold refer?

Although many of us have not faced much—if any—actual physical persecution, we all still face trials, difficulties, and opposition. First Peter teaches us how to handle these trials, difficulties, and opposition by the grace of God. This is why this series is titled *Living in Hostile Territory by the Grace of God.*

Peter suffered a miserable spiritual failure, but he came back to have an effective ministry. He came out as pure gold and ready for God to use him.

We all have spiritual failures, but we, like Peter, do not need to remain in that condition. Christ will welcome us back from failure to serve the Lord effectively. We should make a new start each day of our lives by keeping current with our confession of sin and by telling the Lord each morning that we want to put our sins behind and make a fresh start for Him.

20. How will making a fresh start each day help us to handle the trials of life?

Making It Personal

21. If you have not done so yet today, make a fresh start with the Lord now. If you have not believed on Jesus, make a start with Him by trusting in Him as your personal Savior.

22. What are some steps you can take to come back from spiritual failure to effective ministry?

23. Which of these steps do you need to take right now?

24. Memorize Matthew 4:18 and 19.

Sometimes It Hurts

*Remembering God's care in the midst of trials
helps us to handle them Biblically.*

1 Peter 1:3–12

"That the trial of your faith, being much more precious than of gold that perisheth, though it be tried with fire, might be found unto praise and honor and glory at the appearing of Jesus Christ" (1 Peter 1:7).

The Greeting Card Association publishes greeting card statistics on its Web site, www.greetingcard.org. Consider these facts about greeting cards in the United States:

• Consumers purchase approximately 7 billion greeting cards each year, generating nearly $7.5 billion in retail sales.

• The average person receives more than 20 cards per year.

• Women purchase more than 80 percent of all greeting cards.

• The most popular everyday cards are birthday (60%), anniversary (8%), get well (7%), friendship (6%), and sympathy cards (6%).

• Nine out of 10 Americans say they look forward to receiving personal letters and greeting cards because cards allow them to keep in touch with friends and family and make them feel they are important to someone else.

• Although e-mail, text messaging, and phone calls are valued by Americans for helping them communicate with family and friends, the majority of Americans say they prefer the old-fashioned handwritten card or letter to make someone feel truly special.

Getting Started

1. Describe a time when you were going through a difficulty and received a shower of cards from people.

2. How did the cards help you cope with the problem?

3. How do you think receiving no cards would have affected you?

Peter emphasized God's care for believers as he began his letter. Realizing the many facets of God's care for us in the midst of trials is important to getting through the trial successfully.

Searching the Scriptures

God's Mercy and Care

First Peter 1:2 instructs believers about the election of God, the sanctification of the Spirit, and the sprinkling of Christ's blood. If God had not taken the initiative and acted, there would be no salvation for us. These gracious actions of God grew out of His mercy. The word "according" in verse 3 implies that His mercy *drove* Him to provide salvation. The compelling force of God's merciful heart moved Him to provide salvation for sinners.

4. Read 1 Peter 1:3. How does knowing God's merciful heart drove Him to offer salvation help you to understand God's care for you?

In salvation we are "begotten" (v. 3) or "born again" (v. 23). The word "begotten" means "renewal" or the impartation of new life through the seed of the Word and the ministry of the Holy Spirit. Our priceless salvation, our privileged position as sons of God, and our enjoyment of eternal life did not begin with us, our merit, our discernment, or our better-than-average wisdom, but rather in the abundant, compelling mercy of God. God's mercy makes it impossible for anyone to boast of their own contribution to salvation.

Each person who trusts Christ as Savior is born "unto a living hope." A living, or lively, hope energizes the believer every day. This living, energetic hope has two aspects: it's an attitude of eager anticipation, and it's a blessed assurance. Believers know that the glories of Heaven are ours just as if we were already there, for we are already there—in Christ. The foundation for our hope is "the resurrection of Jesus Christ from [among] the dead," for apart from His death, burial, and resurrection, we have no hope at all.

5. When have you been energized by the living hope in you? What were the circumstances?

Believers' Assured Inheritance

6. Read 1 Peter 1:4. What words did Peter use to describe the permanence of your reserved inheritance in Heaven?

7. Read Psalm 16:5. Who is the focal point of your reserved inheritance in Heaven?

Our Lord has reserved for His children Heaven itself and its inde-scribable eternal city (Revelation 21; 22); the prepared mansions of John 14:1–3; and eternity with Christ, with our saved loved ones, and with the glorious hosts of the redeemed. God has promised rewards at the Bema Seat to those who have lived for Christ. We look forward to glori-fied bodies delivered from weariness, disease, pain, and physical limita-tions, and to hearts free of sorrow.

Since the inheritance has already been set aside by God, it is the most secure deposit in the universe. It can never be destroyed by the enemy, never diminished in value, never polluted, and never wasted away. It is an assured inheritance, which the Lord promises to deliver at full value.

8. Which part of your secure inheritance are you looking forward to the most?

So Great Salvation

In verse 3, "who are kept" refers to those who have been born again, those whose inheritance is reserved in Heaven (v. 4). God con-tinually performs this action in behalf of us who believe. Because of His unbroken care twenty-four hours each day, we believers will be on hand in Heaven to receive our reserved inheritance. The assurance of our inheritance does not in any way depend on our own strength, perfection of life, or determination, but rather on God's strength and purpose.

9. Have you struggled with whether you could lose your salvation? Explain.

10. How should 1 Peter 1:5 help you to rest in the permanency of your salvation?

"Faith" is the channel that relates us believers to the divine power. By faith in the Savior, each believer entered into the divine family. Now by faith also, we believers claim this power of God, acting in our behalf. Even our faith is a gift of God—worked in us by the Holy Spirit through His Word (Romans 10:17)—so that in salvation all boasting is excluded.

The term "salvation" involves several truths. It includes justification (being declared righteous by God), which becomes ours the moment we trust the Savior. "Salvation" also embraces our sanctification—the day-by-day deliverance from the power and dominion of sin in our lives. Peter's statement in verse 5 points to a third aspect of salvation, our glorification. Only at that "last time" will Christians experience the fullness and the wonder of "so great salvation."

11. In summary, how is God's care shown in His provision for your salvation?

12. How could remembering God's provision for salvation help in handling life's trials?

Trials

We will "greatly rejoice" in the "last time" (v. 6), when we are glorified and our salvation is completed. Although we rejoice in our present salvation—and rightly so—yet we shall have unbounded, unlimited rejoicing when our salvation is completed.

Trials are for "now," "for a season," not for eternity. Faith is a present grace, not a grace of Heaven. When faith becomes sight, it is no longer needed. Consequently, any testing of faith must be in the here and now, not in the next life. Life on earth is where we are candidates for problems, but only for a season. At the longest, the time of trial can be only for a lifetime, which in comparison to eternity is almost as nothing.

13. How does knowing trials are limited to life on earth affect your view of trials?

God does not say that everyone needs trials all the time or that all believers will face equal testing. The measure of trials may depend on God's purpose for a particular individual. The Lord of infinite wisdom and love tailors the time, the duration, and the quantity of the trials to fit each of His children. His purpose for some may be greater spheres of usefulness, while for others He may design disciplinary trials to remove sins or to teach correct behavior.

'This Is Simply a Test'

Our trials are tests to determine genuineness and durability. Our trials examine the quality of our faith. It's like a teacher giving a test so the student can prove what he knows and get a good grade. Will faith stand the test of dark days, disappointments, sorrow, criticism, rebuffs, physical pain, and unrecognized service? These are some of the "manifold temptations" Peter referred to in verse 6.

Then Peter said that the testing of one's faith is much more precious than the testing of gold (v. 7). The fiery testing of gold purifies the metal and increases its value. The fiery testing of faith (4:12) is of far greater value because it purifies believers to better reflect the image of Christ. Proven faith outlasts even precious metal, for our successfully overcoming trials will result in praise, honor, and glory to the Lord.

14. Describe a time when you realized the benefits of a trial even though it was difficult to endure.

In verses 3–7, Peter told believers in Christ what salvation includes and then described the trials they would face.

15. Why do you think Peter spoke about salvation before mentioning trials?

16. How is God's care shown even in the midst of trials?

Neither we nor the believers to whom Peter was writing had seen Christ, but this should not change our perspective. We do not have to see Him to love Him and to rejoice in Him. We do these things by faith. To believe only because of what we can see would not be faith (John 20:29; 2 Cor. 5:7).

Because of our relationship with the Savior, we can rejoice in trials rather than be shaken by them. The term "joy unspeakable" means that the joy cannot be expressed in human language. This joy is also "full of glory," or glorified. This kind of joy goes beyond the joy that is typical of life on this earth. This is the kind of joy a believer can have even in trials.

17. How does your relationship with Christ demonstrate God's care?

18. How can that relationship help in handling life's trials?

A Glorious Future

In verse 9 Peter affirmed to his readers that the end, or result, of faith in Christ would be the salvation of their souls. While all believers have salvation the moment they trust Christ as Savior, Peter was referring to the future aspect of salvation, which is the time when believers will finally be with the Lord (Romans 8:18–23; 13:11; 1 John 3:2).

Peter elaborated on the matter of the believer's salvation, saying that the prophets who foretold of the grace that should come occasionally had a difficult time understanding what they were writing about (vv. 10–12). They did research to find out the time and the character of the time relating to the sufferings of Christ and the glory that should follow.

That there would be both suffering and glory was a mystery to the prophets. They could not see how both could happen (vv. 10, 11).

The prophecies about Christ that God revealed to the Old Testament prophets were not intended for their own day but for later generations, those of Peter's day and following (v. 12). But the preaching of the gospel of Jesus Christ, by Holy Spirit-empowered preachers, fulfilled God's intent.

Salvation is so special that even the angels desire to look into it. The good angels never experience the joys of salvation because they are confirmed in their righteous state. Consequently, they are intensely interested in God's plan of salvation for humans.

19. How is God's care shown in the blessings He has promised believers?

20. How could remembering God's future blessings help in handling life's trials?

Trials are going to come into our lives. They are inevitable. In fact, they are for our good and for the praise of God (1 Peter 1:7). However, these benefits can result only if we handle life's trials correctly.

Making It Personal

21. Which of the evidences for God's care have you successfully used to encourage you while going through a trial?

_____ Provision for salvation

_____ Help in trials

_____ Relationship with Christ

_____ Promise of future blessings

22. Which ones will you use to help you through a trial this week?

23. Memorize 1 Peter 1:7.

Not Sinless, but Sinning Less

We should be holy in every area of life because God our Father is holy.

1 Peter 1:13–16

"But as he which hath called you is holy, so be ye holy in all manner of conversation; Because it is written, Be ye holy; for I am holy" (1 Peter 1:15, 16).

If you were on East 60th Street in New York, you might want to stop by Serendipity 3, a famous restaurant known for its Forbidden Broadway Sundae and its Frrrozen Hot Chocolate. And if you had $25,000 to burn, you might try the Frrrozen Haut Chocolate Dessert. Or not! One fact might deter you: In 2007 the restaurant was closed for a month or so after it failed two health inspections in a row. Inspectors had found a live mouse, mouse droppings, fruit flies, house flies, and more than a hundred live cockroaches.

In spite of that "little setback," Serendipity 3 remains a popular place for meals and desserts.

Getting Started

1. How would you react if a restaurant served your meal on a dirty plate?

2. Would you stay in the restaurant and wait for another plate of food, or would you get up and leave?

3. How might this illustration relate to offering ourselves to God for His use?

God expects us to live holy lives. Often we offer ourselves to Him without paying attention to the sins in our lives. Peter wrote about our need to be holy.

Searching the Scriptures

Peter wrote about the living hope we have at salvation (1 Peter 1:3). That living hope should affect our lives, beginning with our minds and then moving to our practice. Starting with verse 13 Peter addressed the effects that a living hope has on our lives.

Be Ready

In Peter's day, men wore long, flowing robes that could get in the way. If a man wanted to do strenuous work or a quick activity, he would lift the bottom of his robe and tuck it into his belt (1 Kings 18:46; 2 Kings 4:29; John 13:4, 5; 21:7). Since the belt went around the loins (or waist), this action was called "girding up the loins."

Peter applied this custom to the minds of believers. We believers are to gird up our minds, or prepare our thought processes for action. As we focus on Christ's return (the living hope), we will not focus on many of the world's distractions.

4. What are some of the worldly focuses a believer might be tempted to fix his mind on?

5. Read Philippians 4:8. What connection do you see between thoughts and actions in this verse?

Getting our minds focused on Christ and His return will shape our attitudes first and then our actions. Peter was well aware of this truth when he called for his readers to gird up the loins of their minds.

Be Disciplined

While "sober" includes abstinence from any intoxicating beverage, Peter surely meant more than that in verse 13. There the word refers to the self-control that will keep believers from intoxication with any sinful indulgence or excess. God makes self-discipline, or self-control, possible for us by giving us His Spirit. The Spirit helps us as we yield to Him.

6. Read Ephesians 5:18. Is yielding to the Spirit something that comes effortlessly to a believer? Explain.

Be Looking

The expression "to the end" in verse 13 could be translated "completely." The idea of the phrase "hope to the end" is that we are to set our hope completely on the grace of God, which will be brought to us at the revelation of Jesus Christ. We are already recipients of His grace, but there is a sense in which that grace which brings salvation will be culminated at the appearing of Christ. Peter encouraged his readers to set their hope completely on the return of Christ.

Be ready, be disciplined, and be looking—these serve as three prerequisites for holiness.

Be Holy

God commands His children to be holy (vv.14, 15). As Peter communicated God's command, he called the readers "obedient children" because they had obeyed the truth in the past. Peter was urging them to continual obedience in this matter of holiness.

God has given many positive commands, things His people must do. He also has given many negative commands, things His people must not do. God knows that to have positive holiness, the negatives must be addressed.

Negative Aspects

Holiness involves being set apart for God in our attitudes and behaviors. The things God calls out of bounds must be avoided, and the things God prescribes must be accepted. Scripture says we "put off" and "put on" (Col. 3:8–14). Holiness is both a negative and positive action that extends to every area of our lives.

7. Read 1 Peter 1:14. What is the negative command in this verse?

8. What are some specific attitudes and actions believers should "put off"?

Peter said that we must not "fashion" ourselves according to the desires of our former or pre-salvation days (v. 14). This word (not fashioning) appears only one other time in Scripture: Romans 12:2, where it is translated "be not conformed." The idea in 1 Peter and Romans is that the unsaved people of this world have a certain shape, style, or pattern of living, which believers must avoid. (Of course, behind this is Satan, who wants to lead men to sin.) Believers should not let themselves be shaped or patterned by the world. Just as a piece of clay will take the shape of a mold, so many Christians take the shape of the world because they fail to recognize or counteract its pressures.

No one will resist the pattern of the world by merely wishing for victory. If we do nothing to prevent it, we will become like the world.

We must actively resist that mold in order to avoid it.

9. How fruitful will we be as believers if we see ourselves as a helpless lump of clay that is unable to resist the world's influence?

The pattern of the world contradicts God's revealed will at many points. We need to resist its unholiness in the way we think, the things we value, and the manner in which we act. We must combat the influence of the world's sinful desires upon ourselves!

There is a sense in which our former sinful lusts and deeds were committed "in ignorance," according to 1 Peter 1:14. This does not excuse us, but the truth of the matter is that we had no desire or ability for holiness. Our nature was sinful, so we could not do anything differently. We were ignorant of how to please God.

Positive Aspects

Not only must believers stop doing certain things in order to be holy, but we must also do something positively. "Be ye holy in all manner of conversation" (v. 15). In sharp contrast to being fashioned after pre-salvation desires (former lusts), God provides a new standard for believers.

For the Christian, holiness has more than one aspect. Positionally we are already sanctified, set apart or holy (1 Corinthians 1:2; Hebrews 10:14). In Christ, and with the Holy Spirit dwelling within, we have a holy standing before the Judge of the universe. That holiness should now be demonstrated in all our conduct.

10. Read Hebrews 10:14. What is the time limit on the positional sanctification that God grants to believers?

What does holiness look like practically? The word "holiness" has the root idea of being "set apart." In the Old Testament certain clothes, vessels, days, and so on were considered holy. This did not mean there was anything inherently better about one vessel than another. It simply meant that those vessels were set apart for use in things that pertained to God.

This is the idea of our practical holiness. We set ourselves apart from the sinful things of the world so we God can use us. If we are defiled with uncleanness, we will not be of much use to Him. Holiness is a life of victory over sin. It is a life of purity and separation from evil. It is living like Christ.

11. What are some of the positive attitudes and actions you must "put on"?

12. Which aspect of holiness—positive or negative—do you find easiest to focus on? Why?

13. What might result from an imbalanced view of holiness?

Admittedly, holiness goes contrary to self-centered human nature. We want to serve and please ourselves.

14. How would you describe the struggle within you between following the world's influence and striving for holiness?

How Holy?

The question may arise, How holy must I be? The Scriptures answer this very clearly.

15. Read 1 Peter 1:15. What limits, if any, does this verse give on the extent of holiness in a believer's life?

God desires holiness in all that we do. Holiness on the personal level means that we must be holy and set apart for God in the area of our thoughts. We must avoid the philosophies of the world (negatively stated) and fill our minds with God-honoring concepts (positively stated). We must evaluate ideas by the standard of God's revealed truth. The messages of the entertainment media, our neighbors, politicians, society's opinion makers, printed and electronic news—all must be put through the grid of God's Word before we accept them. When we learn to obey Biblical principles of separation to God, we can make proper judgments about contemporary matters that the Bible does not directly address.

The command for holiness demands that we live our lives for God in every area and that we separate from all evil. We never outgrow our need for holiness.

In verse 15, Peter reminded believers that our God is holy. He is separate or set apart from all that is sinful. His nature cannot accept sin. He does only what is right. Some have said that holiness may be the foundational attribute of God, that it forms the basis for all the rest of His character. He never violates His holiness in any of His plans or work.

16. Read 1 Peter 1:16. What is the believer's motivation for being holy?

"Be ye holy for I am holy," is a citation from Moses (Leviticus 11:44). God is the One Who has called us to salvation (2 Timothy 1:9), and He is holy. We are therefore to be holy as well.

Some may read this and say, "I cannot be holy like God. He is perfect, but I fail so often." This is true for all of us. However, Peter did not say to be holy "like" or "as" God is holy. He told us to be holy "for" or "because" God is holy. We can never match God's holiness, for His is a divine, perfect holiness. We as redeemed creatures are to be holy because our Father is holy.

A father could say to a son about to have a vaccination, "Son, be brave like Daddy." By this he would not mean to be just as brave as the father is. He is rather saying that the son should model himself after his father and, within his own range of possibility, be brave. We will not be holy to the degree God is holy, but we are to be holy because our Father is holy.

Let's take this one step farther. To what extent is God holy? He is holy in every area. How holy should we be then? We should be holy in every area of our lives. Verse 16 is not so much about the kind of holiness as it is about the extent of holiness.

17. How will living a holy life will help you accomplish the overall theme of 1 Peter of handling your trials correctly by God's grace?

Making It Personal

18. What are some areas of your life in which you have need for greater holiness?

19. What steps do you need to take to become more holy in your daily living?

20. Spend some time in silent prayer, confessing sin and asking for the Lord's help to be victorious, to avoid sin, and to put something positive in its place.

21. Memorize 1 Peter 1:15 and 16.

Loving Fervently

A believer's fear for God is shown in his love for fellow believers.

1 Peter 1:17–25

"Seeing ye have purified your souls in obeying the truth through the Spirit unto unfeigned love of the brethren, see that ye love one another with a pure heart fervently" (1 Peter 1:22).

You have heard of the Wright brothers, but did you know the boys had a younger sister? When Wilbur and Orville were making it big, their sister Katharine was just as popular and well-known as they were. In fact, she was awarded the French Legion of Honour and was considered "the third Wright brother." It was her life savings that kept the brothers afloat while they experimented with their flying machines. It was she who tutored them on the mathematics of aerodynamics. It was she who had the business sense and marketed them and their machines. Katharine also designed and sewed fabric to cover wings for their experimental aircraft. Someone has said, "Katharine was their strength and support. She abandoned her life unselfishly and completely to her brothers."

Getting Started

1. What are some of the blessings of having brothers and sisters in Christ?

2. How will someone who truly values his brothers and sisters in Christ demonstrate that value?

Today we will be examining doctrinal truths about God our Father, Christ Jesus, our salvation, and our Bible. But we are also going to be looking at this important matter of our relationships with fellow believers.

Searching the Scriptures

Fear the Lord

Peter said we are to "pass" (v. 17), or "conduct ourselves," in a certain manner while we are on earth.

3. Read 1 Peter 1:17. How is a believer supposed to pass the time of his stay on earth?

4. Does that answer seem odd to you? Explain.

The "fear" in this verse refers to our fear of God.

5. What thoughts does the phrase "fear God" bring to your mind?

The fear of God is an attitude of awe and reverent respect for the Judge of all the earth, the holy and infinite God, not a cringing emotion of cowardice.

As we fear God while on earth, we should order, or arrange, the time of our daily lives with a two-part objective: first, of pleasing Christ and, then, of bearing a good witness to those around us. We should also realize that such a lifestyle will mark us as "sojourners," or foreigners, in the eyes of the unsaved.

The Father's Judgment

To those who know Christ as Savior, God is both Father and the God Who "judgeth according to every man's work" (v. 17). He is impartial, "without respect of persons." God does not judge by appearance, for He looks on the heart (1 Samuel 16:7). The word used for "judge" speaks of a testing to approve what one finds. The emphasis or thought is that God as Father is looking for things that He may praise in us.

Lesson 3 points out that God's people are to be holy because He is holy. First Peter 1:17 adds another dimension: those who have been born into God's family by faith in Jesus Christ should live to please Him and seek His approval as their Father and their Judge.

6. What did your parents' approval mean to you as you were growing up?

7. What did they do to show their approval of you?

8. How does God show His approval of you when He recognizes your respectful obedience to Him?

The Son's Sacrifice

To be redeemed is to be purchased from sin by the payment of a price. The price was not some temporal, corruptible thing, like the money used in purchasing slaves. In God's law, almost all redemption was by blood (Hebrews 9:22), from the covering of the nakedness of Adam and Eve with the skins of slain animals to the thousands of animals sacrificed at the tabernacle and the temple.

9. Read 1 Peter 1:19. What purchased your redemption?

The final sacrifice of God's Son at Calvary fulfilled those Old Testament pictures; for Jesus Christ offered Himself, the Lamb of God, as the final and truly effective bloody sacrifice for sin.

In 1 Peter 1:19, blood points to a sacrificial death. It is precious because of the Person giving His life, because of the purpose of His sacrifice, and because of the product obtained—sinners brought into the family of God.

10. Why should Christ's sacrifice on the cross for our redemption cause us to respect God?

The high cost of our redemption provides a proper motivation for the careful ordering of our attitudes, thoughts and activities to please God.

Believers' Faith and Hope in God's Plan

The Christian's faith is built on the firmest possible foundation. Our faith and hope are in God (v. 21). From the very beginning, God had our salvation in view. He laid the plan, provided the means, and finally signified His approval of Christ's work by raising His Son from the dead and placing Him at His right hand in Glory.

Note these expressions. Christ's work was "foreordained" (v. 20). Man's sin did not take God by surprise. He had foreseen it and planned the remedy. Christ "was manifest . . . for you," coming to earth to do the work for our benefit (v. 20). Christ was "raised" from among the dead ones (v. 21). This was God's indication of His satisfaction with the payment of sin's penalty. Christ's resurrection is our guarantee of resurrection (Romans 8:11).

11. With such an assured and glorious future, why do you think believers would be content to live anything less than holy lives?

Love Fellow Believers

12. Read 1 Peter 1:22. In light of the truths about God's work in our behalf, God expects you to fear Him (v. 17). What else does God expect from you in light of the truths about His work?

13. What two qualities should characterize believers' love for each other?

14. List two synonyms for each of those qualities.

How does a person express the new life in Christ? The Word of God points to brotherly love as one evidence of personal faith in Jesus Christ (John 13:35). Peter admonished believers, "See that ye love one another with a pure heart fervently" (1 Peter 1:22). We are to love other Christians because God loves them, and we are to love them unselfishly and with long-suffering, patience, and kindness (1 Corinthians 13:4–8). "Fervently" in 1 Peter 1:22 means "with a warm spirit" and also "with full intensity, not holding back something." Here is an admonition appropriate for every generation of believers.

15. Do you love your fellow believers fervently and with a pure heart? List specific evidence for your answer.

16. What restrictions, if any, does God put on exactly which fellow believers you are supposed to love (1 Peter 1:22)?

Obedience to the Truth

The believers to whom Peter was writing had obeyed the true gospel message, and the Holy Spirit had used that obedience to purify their souls: "Seeing ye have purified your souls" (v. 22). One result of their obedience was that they had an "unfeigned love of the brethren." An unfeigned love is a real love without hypocrisy, not just a show of love, but a genuine work from the heart. The purifying of the Word had produced a family affection of Christians for each other.

17. Describe a time when someone showed you genuine love.

18. What did the person's love mean to you?

The Christians who read this letter already had a fondness for fellow believers because of their faith in Christ. Peter was urging them to take the next step of showing sacrificial love.

19. What are some ways that you can show sacrificial love to fellow believers?

New Birth

A person enters the human family by means of physical birth, and enters the divine family only by a supernatural, spiritual birth: "Not of blood, nor of the will of the flesh, nor of the will of man, but of God" (John 1:13). The form of the verb "being born again" (1 Peter 1:23) speaks of a single, decisive act in the past with a continuous result. In other words, a person is born again at one time and continues in that condition forever. There is no Scriptural foundation for the concept that one can or need be born again spiritually more than once, just as there is no scientific foundation for the concept that we can be born physically many times.

The new birth is "not of corruptible seed" (v. 23). All earthly seed—whether it be human, animal, or plant—is subject to decay and can reproduce only that which eventually decays. The new life resulting from the new birth is eternal and spiritual because it is the product of (1) the sacrifice of Christ as the price (1:18, 19); (2) the incorruptible Word of God as the seed (1:23; Luke 8:11); and (3) the Spirit of God as the agent (John 3:5, 6). Because the seed of salvation is the Word of God "which liveth and abideth for ever" (1 Peter 1:23), the product of that seed, spiritual life through faith in Christ, possesses the same eternal qualities.

20. Since all believers are born again and possess eternal life, how should that fact affect your love for them?

A person's life on earth is infinitely brief compared to eternity. Peter expressed the idea quite graphically, saying that all flesh is like grass (v. 24). Can we afford to waste this brief opportunity by not loving our brethren or by harboring attitudes utterly foreign to a child of God?

21. Read 1 Peter 1:24. How should the briefness of life affect your love for fellow believers?

In sharp contrast to the finite and decaying nature of all things around us, the Word of the Lord lives, abides, and endures forever (vv. 23, 25). God has preserved His Word from all human attempts to destroy it. God also preserves the product of His Word (believers) from all attempts of the enemy to snatch them out of His hand (John 10:28–30). Believers are "kept by the power of God" (1 Peter 1:5).

Making It Personal

22. How does fearing the Lord help you in trials?

23. How does loving fellow believers help you in trials?

24. What are some excuses you might give for not fearing God in trials?

25. What are some excuses you might give for not loving others while you experience trials?

26. What act of Christian love will you show to someone this week? To whom?

27. Memorize 1 Peter 1:22.

Declaring His Praises

Believers can declare God's praises because He has saved and nurtured us and because He honors us with a unique position and relationship.

1 Peter 2:1–12

"But ye are a chosen generation, a royal priesthood, an holy nation, a peculiar people; that ye should shew forth the praises of him who hath called you out of darkness into his marvellous light" (1 Peter 2:9).

Sports writers seem to like the phrase "singing his praises" or something close to it, when they write about popular, winning coaches—especially if there's some way to tie it in to real singing. For instance, take Thayer Evans, whose article on Texas Christian University Coach Gary Patterson is titled "T.C.U. Fans Are Singing Football Coach's Praises." The article begins by summarizing Coach Patterson's one-time singing career. And then there's Dan Raley, who wrote about Washington State University's basketball coach Tony Bennett. Get it? (Tony Bennett was a popular, award-winning singer in the 1950s to early '70s, who also had a comeback and is still popular among many today.) Raley titled his article, "WSU coach Bennett has 'em singing his praises." But the gist of both articles is that Bennett and Patterson are praiseworthy coaches.

Getting Started

1. What do we mean by this figure of speech "singing his praises"?

2. Whose praises would you like to sing? Why?

From 1 Peter 2:1–12 we will discover several responsibilities of believers. One of these is declaring God's praises because He has saved and nurtured us and because He honors us with a unique position and relationship.

Searching the Scriptures

Lay aside Sin

3. Read 1 Peter 2:1. Do the sins in this list affect more than just the person committing them? Explain.

4. How do these sins fit into God's desire for believers to love one another (1 Peter 1:22)?

Christians have entered a new life designed to display holy conduct and sincere love for spiritual brothers and sisters.

In 1 Peter 2:1, Peter named certain attitudes and actions that are completely incompatible with our new life. As born again ones, we must lay aside "all malice" (wickedness or evil conduct), "all guile" (deceit or hypocritical acts), and "all evil speakings" (slandering or running down another individual). These negatives displease God. We cannot "love one another . . . fervently" while entertaining attitudes or actions contrary to our spiritual family.

Desire the Word

5. Read 1 Peter 2:2 and 3. Describe a newborn baby's desire for his mother's milk. How is that desire demonstrated?

6. What specific comparisons can you draw for believers who are to desire the Word "as newborn babes"?

On the positive side, believers are to "desire the sincere milk of the word." As a hungry baby cries out for nourishment, so every Christian should manifest an intense appetite for food, in this case, the genuine Word of God. A person who tolerates sin in his life will find himself lacking interest in a menu of God's Word. This may explain why some people have so little longing for the Word.

Peter concluded this section of his letter by saying that believers should do these things "if so be ye have tasted that the Lord is gracious" (v. 3). Peter was saying that his readers should obey these commands since they had been saved and had found out that the Lord is gracious ("if" carries the sense of "since" in the sentence). When we have tasted God's grace by experience, we find out that He satisfies, and that assurance prompts our holy living.

7. How does being a growing Christian declare God's praises?

Living Stones

8. Read 1 Peter 2:5. What comes to your mind when you read that believers are "living stones"?

Peter called these believers "living stones" because he was talking about them as a part of a building, a spiritual house. Just as stones are used to construct physical houses, living stones make up God's spiritual house, also called the church and the Body of Jesus Christ (Ephesians 1:22, 23). Believers are called "living stones" because they are living people, not rocks or bricks.

The "you also" of 1 Peter 2:5 includes all believers scattered throughout the five Roman provinces as part of the spiritual house, and by extension, refers to believers today. Although far removed from their brothers and sisters in Jerusalem, Peter's readers were still part of a great spiritual family and needed to sense their spiritual unity with believers everywhere.

9. What can we learn about our relationship with each other by being called "living stones" connected in one building?

A spiritual house must have a foundation that matches the nature of the superstructure. Quoting from Isaiah 28:16, Peter spoke of Christ as the "chief corner stone" and "the head of the corner." His building will not fall or fail, for it is built on the eternal Rock (Matthew 16:18).

A Rejected Stone

Christ was "disallowed indeed" by the leaders of Israel because He did not measure up to what they expected (John 1:11). They rejected His claims in spite of the strongest evidence in miracles and teachings. Some individuals did accept and praise the Stone, but the nation rejected Him.

God's evaluation of His Son is quite different. From before the creation of the world Jesus Christ was the elect and precious, cocreator with the Father and the Spirit, the channel of God's salvation, the head of a new family, and the foundation stone for the church, "chosen of God, and precious" (1 Peter 2:4).

A Chief Cornerstone

Christ is not just one of many possible cornerstones: He is the only Cornerstone. Paul taught the same concept in Ephesians 2:20. Christ is both the solid rock foundation on which the whole superstructure is erected, and the stone that unites and holds together all the "living stones."

10. Read 1 Peter 2:6. Why is it important for churches to know that Jesus, the Cornerstone, holds together the believers, the "living stones"?

A Precious Stone

In verse 6 we see Christ as elect and precious to God. Because God is pleased with His Son, those in union with the Son by faith shall never be "confounded," or put to shame. No enemy shall arise who can sever us from that union we have with the Chief Stone of the spiritual house. Our place is secure in the elect and precious Son.

While the Son is precious to the Father (vv. 4, 6), in verse 7 we see that He is also precious to the believer. His preciousness is recognized and appreciated only by those who believe in Him. For the "disobedient" (disbelieving), there is no recognition of His love and mercy, no reception of His gracious forgiveness, no participation in His gift of eternal life, and no place in His spiritual house.

11. What does your life say about Jesus? Do you demonstrate by your choices that Jesus is "precious"?

An Honored Stone

Since the rulers of Israel could not see beauty in this Stone, they marked Him as rejected or unfit for their use. God disagreed with Israel's verdict: "The stone . . . disallowed [rejected] . . . is made the head of the corner," wrote Peter in verse 7. After Israel rejected Christ, God raised Him and honored Him by placing Him at His own right hand.

A Judging Stone

"A stone of stumbling" in verse 8 refers to Christ as an obstacle against which the unbelieving kick. A "rock of offense" pictures Christ as a ledge or a solid rock over which the unbeliever trips. No doubt this "stone of stumbling" and "rock of offense" related especially to unbelieving Israel's view of Christ, but Peter made the reference broader in scope by stating "even to them which stumble [are scandalized] at the word." The disobedient or unbelieving resist the person of Christ and the Word of God. Eventually the Stone Himself will become their Judge.

12. How does our being "living stones" of His church declare God's praises?

Individual Priests

The priests of the Old Testament were to be holy, clean, and without blemish, but they were limited in number. Under the New Covenant all believers are members of the priesthood and thus should be holy—separated to God and clean.

The pastor behind the pulpit and the believer in the pew are equally priests before God. God has more specific standards for church leadership than for church fellowship (Acts 6:1–3; 1 Timothy 3:1–13); but in the matter of the priesthood, He clearly sets forth standards of cleanness and separateness for all believers.

13. Have you ever thought that since you weren't a pastor you could

get away with a few sins here and there? How does being called a "priest" change your perspective?

The church is something new, "a chosen generation" (v. 9), or elect people from every tribe, tongue, and nation who are born into a new family by spiritual generation, or new birth. Believers are then a "royal priesthood." This combination of duty and privilege was unknown in the Old Testament. The Levitical priests were not kings, and the Davidic kings were not priests. But in Christ, believers are made both kings and priests (Revelation 1:6). As priests we worship and seek to bring men to God and make God known to men. As kings we demonstrate the character of the King of Kings by submission to His rule over our lives.

14. Read 1 Peter 2:9 and 10. What would you say to the believer whose goal in life is to promote himself to gain all he can of this world's riches and recognition?

As Peter wrote, Israel had failed as a nation and was being scattered. God was creating a new nation of believers, having no geographical boundaries, earthly capital, or human government.

"A peculiar people" (still in verse 9) means "a people for His own possession," not strange or odd people. Our distinguishing marks are not some strange style of dress or other physical badge. Rather, God has purchased us for Himself, and we reflect His ownership.

15. How does our being "a royal priesthood" declare God's praises?

Pilgrims

16. Read 1 Peter 2:11. If you were sent to a foreign country to live

for three months, what would be your mindset in regard to the new culture around you? Would you seek to embrace it and immerse yourself in it? Explain.

Peter called believers "strangers and pilgrims" on the earth. "Stranger" describes those who have no rights or legal status, while "pilgrim" defines those who are only temporary dwellers. Our citizenship is in Heaven where we will reside forever. We are living in a foreign land while on earth. That fact should keep us from becoming attached to this world and from seeking to embrace its values.

As citizens of a heavenly country, we act as ambassadors of our King during our temporary residence on earth. We ought to display characteristics that speak well of our heavenly Home. One behavior that will certainly mark the Christian as a representative of a different realm is to abstain from fleshly lusts. To "abstain" in verse 11 means to hold back constantly. "Fleshly lusts" speaks of strong desires that are both typical of the flesh and contrary to God's holiness.

Fleshly lusts "war against the soul." They wage a destructive campaign against a person's spiritual nature. God holds each believer responsible to abstain from fleshly lusts. Curbing one's fleshly appetite creates a climate favorable for spiritual growth.

Another mark of our heavenly citizenship is to keep our "conversation," or behavior, honest (v. 12). "Honest" speaks of a visible goodness. Our Christian conduct or manner of life is honest when our outward conduct accurately reflects what we have been made in Christ.17.

17. How does our being pilgrims here on earth declare God's praises?

This section of God's Word reveals that we are to grow as Christians by desiring the Word of God. It shows that we are living stones in a spiritual house of which Christ is the Foundation and Cornerstone. It teaches that we are priests who have certain responsibilities and we are pilgrims here who need to abstain from the lusts of the world.

Making It Personal

18. What are some of the excellent things God does?

19. What are some ways of communicating to people the excellencies of God?

20. How will this action help us handle our trials?

21. Write a prayer of praise to God for the excellent things He has done in their lives.

22. Memorize 1 Peter 2:9.

Submit? . . . Me?

God desires for believers to submit to those
who are in authority over them.

1 Peter 2:13–20

"Submit yourselves to every ordinance of man for the Lord's sake. . . . Servants, be subject to your masters with all fear; not only to the good and gentle, but also to the froward" (1 Peter 2:13, 18).

What makes a bad boss? That's what David Molpus, former national workplace correspondent for National Public Radio, wanted to know. More than three hundred listeners responded with e-mails within two days of his request. Here are a few descriptions of bad bosses: being a Jekyll-and-Hyde boss who is your best friend one day and your worst enemy the next; showering criticism while stinting on praise; berating successful workers so they don't get "a big head"; duplicitous, double-dealing, and hypocritical; using others to deflect their own weaknesses; insensitive; unavailable; unfriendly. Of course, the list could go on and on.

Getting Started

1. What characterized the most difficult boss you have had?

2. How did you respond to him or her?

Submitting to your boss may seem like something God wouldn't care about, but He actually gives us specific instructions about it. Today we are going to look at the matter of authority and our need to submit to those over us as a means of obeying God.

Searching the Scriptures

Submission to Government

3. Read 1 Peter 2:13. When you read the word "submit," do you have a positive or negative reaction?

4. What is the reason for your reaction?

"Submit yourselves" means to bring yourself under the authority of something. The word in 1 Peter 2:13 is closely related to the "be subject" of Romans 13:1. Believers are to comply with the laws of the government. Biblical submission includes both the acts of obedience and the attitude of willingness.

5. Have you ever submitted to the government in action but not in attitude?

6. What were the circumstances?

The Christian's submission is to apply "to every ordinance of man."

In general, the exercise of authority in governmental institutions is in harmony with God's design for the ordering of human life (Romans 13:1–7).

7. Read Romans 13:1 and 2. Why does God take submitting to authorities so seriously?

Why this submission? According to 1 Peter 2:13, it is "for the Lord's sake." Our submission to human authority should not originate merely duty or fear of punishment, but from our standing as children of God. We desire the approval of Heaven, so we submit for Jesus' sake.

8. How does submitting "for the Lord's sake" affect your desire to submit to authorities?

9. Read 1 Peter 2:13 and 14. What different levels of rulers are mentioned, and how does that structure of authority apply to today?

10. What is the purpose of leaders (v. 14)?

List of Authorities

Peter provided a list that, although limited, seems intended to be inclusive of all properly constituted authorities. It begins with kings— those who stand in the highest position of responsible authority—and moves to other rulers who serve under the commission of the king. Rulers at all levels derive their authority from God and represent God, the

Judge. These authorities are responsible for the order of society, punishing those who disobey, and commending those who do well. Such governmental officers should exercise their authority always considering that they themselves are answerable to God.

Peter did not say that we should submit only to good rulers. In fact, in Peter's day Nero, who severely persecuted Christians, was the ruler! God requires that we submit, for His sake, to any ruler.

A point does come at which a Christian must disobey the ruler. That point comes when the government asks him to do something contrary to God's command. Otherwise, a believer who disobeys the government must be prepared to suffer consequences.

11. Read Acts 5:29. What clear instruction does this verse give about choosing between obeying God and obeying men?

Muzzle the Critics

God wills that His followers have an influence on unsaved people around them by their abstinence from fleshly lusts, by honest behavior, by obedience to laws, and by submission to properly constituted authority. According to 1 Peter 2:15, the outcome of such Christian conduct is to silence or muzzle the criticisms of individuals who lack spiritual understanding.

12. Read 1 Peter 2:15. How will obeying authorities put to silence the ignorance of foolish men?

"Not using your liberty for a cloak" in verse 16 repudiates the philosophy of those who pervert liberty into an excuse to harm someone else. Christians are free—free from the bondage and condemnation of the law, free from fear, and free from slavery to the flesh. But Christians are to exercise their freedom in the framework of being God's servants who delight to please their Master. This is the only true freedom. Those who demand freedom from all restraint have already become slaves to their own demands.

13. Read 1 Peter 3:17. What relationships are covered in this verse?

14. Which instruction is the foundation for the other three?

To "honour all men" is to esteem others because they are also creatures of God's creative wisdom and the objects of His love and care, even though their spiritual/moral nature is sorely twisted and fallen.

"Love the brotherhood" admonishes Christians not only to love one another as individuals, but also to love believers as a group. Followers of Christ should demonstrate love for the assembly of believers, the local church. Every member of Christ's Body, not merely our personal friends, qualifies as an object of brotherly love.

To "fear God" means to reverence Him, to respect Him, to stand in humble awe of His holiness, His creatorship, and all of His other qualities in which He is infinitely superior to us. To fear God is to possess a keen sensitivity against anything that would displease Him.

Peter regarded honoring the king as so significant that he declared this admonition at the beginning of his instructions on Christian behavior and repeated it at the end. The One Who is the Source of all authority deserves our honor even more than the king does.

15. What are some ways in which believers need to submit to the government?

Submission to Employers

16. Read 1 Peter 2:18. In what settings are you a "servant" who must answer to a "master"?

In verse 18, "servants" refers to household servants and probably includes both free men and purchased slaves. Slaves were quite numerous in the Roman provinces and comprised a large proportion of the early Christian community. Such a slave-master relationship does not exist in many parts of the world today. However, the employee-employer relationship is somewhat equivalent. The command of verse 18 is for the slave (employee) to be subject to or to submit to his master (employer). He is to rank himself under him, just as every believer should do in relation to the government (v. 13).

Christian servants (employees) are to honor their masters (employers) "with all fear" (with due respect) because they recognize that their masters' authority comes from God and because they reverence God.

17. Read Colossians 3:22. Why is being consistent in our submission to our employers so important?

18. What are some ways an employee might mistreat an unfair employer?

19. Does verse 18 give the mistreated employee the right to take any of those actions? Explain.

The "masters" of verse 18 were full owners and could exercise absolute control over their servants. Some were kind, even though unsaved; others were unfair and made life miserable for their Christian slaves.

20. Read 1 Peter 2:19. What did Peter say is thankworthy?

Peter praised the attitude of the servant who willingly submits himself to the master. Because of his personal reverence for God, such a Christian does not rebel, complain, or cowardly cringe, but submits to his servant position. For a slave to rebel and become bitter toward his master would be natural. Peter said it is the meek and forgiving spirit in spite of unjust treatment that is worthy of thanks or praise (v. 19).

Conscience toward God

The phrase "for conscience toward God" in verse 19 speaks of an awareness of God's presence and will and of a desire to be approved by Him. This outlook explains why the Christian slave's attitude is so different from the normal reaction of the unconverted. Words such as "submit," "endure," "be subject," and "take it patiently" are quite foreign to the flesh.

Each of us can recall occasions when our conduct has merited rebuke. Patience at times when we receive the punishment we deserve has no special merit. But imagine being "buffeted," knocked around," or otherwise made to suffer when you have done what is right and are not at fault. God says that patience in such a situation is "acceptable" or commendable in His eyes.

21. What are some ways in which believers should submit to their employers?

Making It Personal

22. How can a submissive spirit help you handle life's trials?

23. Select one area in which you will begin to submit to the government and/or to your employer.

24. Memorize 1 Peter 2:13 and 18.

Jesus, Example of Submission

Jesus is our primary example of submission and suffering.

1 Peter 2:21–25

"For even hereunto were ye called: because Christ also suffered for us, leaving us an example, that ye should follow his steps" (1 Peter 2:21).

Whether we like it or not, we all adopt certain characteristics and habits of our parents. We pick up their quirky phrases like "What time are you getting around?" and "Do you think money grows on trees?" We also pick up some of their interesting rituals like tucking their pajama pants into their socks before going to bed. Unfortunately we tend to adopt some of our parents' bad habits too. Chewing fingernails or smacking lips while eating are some common ones.

We all must at some point in our lives face the fact that we became our parents. All their idiosyncrasies and annoying habits are now a part of who we are and have or will become part of our children's lives.

Getting Started

1. What do you do or say that is exactly like your mom or dad did

or said while you were growing up?

2. In what ways have your children followed your example?

3. If you have young children, in what areas do you hope your children don't follow your example?

Jesus is our example in many ways. Peter presents Christ as our example for how to respond to suffering, especially suffering for doing what is right. Today's lesson will focus on Christ's example of suffering.

Searching the Scriptures

A Call to Suffering

4. Read 1 Peter 2:20 and 21. In these verses, what did Peter say believers are called to?

God never promised a life of comfort and ease to obedient believers. He makes it clear that living for Him will involve some suffering. Yet in that suffering God will graciously give us peace and comfort so we might be able to bear the suffering.

No one should ever conclude that a suffering believer must be a sinning believer. While God does use painful circumstances to chasten us in our sins, He also brings us suffering as we live for Him. Peter was not discouraged by this fact.

5. Read Acts 5:40 and 41. What attitude did Peter (one of the apostles in these verses) have toward suffering for the sake of Christ?

We, like Peter, should see suffering for the sake of Christ as a reason to rejoice. For suffering for Christ means we are following closely the footprints Jesus left for us (1 Pet. 2:21).

6. How can believers follow closely upon Christ's steps (v. 21)?

God will not call us to walk through the same degree of suffering Christ experienced, but studying His example will help us know how to respond to the suffering we do experience.

The Example of Christ's Suffering

Peter gave us five insights into Christ's suffering.

First, Jesus Christ "did no sin." When Isaiah penned the words "did no sin," they were prophetic. But for Peter, they were observation. Peter had known Christ intimately, so he could give authoritative, firsthand testimony that no matter what the temptations or testing of Satan, his Lord never sinned in word or deed. Isaiah's prophecy indeed came true.

If Christ, the sinless One, could suffer for doing right, then we, sinners saved by grace, should not be surprised when we suffer for Christ's sake.

7. How might this characteristic of Christ translate into your life?

8. What are some sins believers might be tempted to commit as they suffer for Christ's sake?

Second, Christ is our example of complete honesty in circumstances that tempt men to compromise. He put no guile or double meaning in His teachings even though He could have veiled His hard or convicting messages in language that would have appeased His enemies. Sins of the lips are much more subtle than sinful deeds, but even in this area, Christ was guiltless.

Christ's honesty was not just an appearance of honesty. He wasn't a good actor who could fool people into thinking He was honest. He was completely honest from the depths of His heart every moment He was on the earth.

Christ's honesty is what eventually led to His crucifixion. He spoke the truth about Himself, and the Jewish leaders hated Him for it.

9. Read Matthew 26:63–66. What truths did Jesus tell about Himself that the Sanhedrin found to be blasphemous and worthy of death?

Third, Jesus Christ "reviled not again" when He was reviled. He displayed amazing, patient silence rather than loud protest when subjected to undeserved treatment. Isaiah beautifully pictured this when he wrote prophetically, "he openeth not his mouth" (Isaiah 53:7).

10. What takes more strength when being falsely accused: a loud protest or patient silence?

11. Read Matthew 27:12–14. How did Pilate react to Jesus' silent response to the accusations of the chief priests and elders?

Jesus' example teaches us to be patient with those who persecute us so that we might have the opportunity to win them for Christ. Our goal should never be to clamor loudly for our rights, but to maintain a good testimony of loving patience.

Fourth, "he threatened not." Jesus Christ could have called angels to come instantaneously to strike down His enemies, but He did not even intimidate His executioners with threats of judgment (Matthew 26:53, 54).

12. Read Luke 18:10. What did Peter try to do when the soldiers came to arrest Jesus in the Garden before Jesus' trial and eventual crucifixion?

13. Read Matthew 26:51–53 and Luke 22:50 and 51. What did Jesus do to show that He was approaching His coming suffering with a non-threatening attitude?

Instead of threats, Jesus prayed for those who crucified Him. He cared deeply for the people who abused Him and brought Him excruciating pain.

14. Read Luke 23:34. What did Jesus ask the Father to do for those who crucified Him?

Jesus' love for people is greater than His love for Himself. That love led Him to the cross with a nonthreatening manner. When treated wrongly, we, too need to focus on our love for those who mistreat us rather than on our love for ourselves.

Fifth, Jesus Christ "committed himself." He literally handed over Himself to the Father. He knew the Father, and He knew God's righteous judgment. Therefore, Christ could trust the Father to accomplish His good will even in the most painful trial.

15. Read Romans 12:17–20. What admonitions in this passage did Jesus live out?

We must not make securing fairness our primary goal in life. God will take care of the unfairness in the world in His final judgment.

We, like Jesus, should trust God to judge righteously those who mistreat us. If we feel compelled to take up our own cause, we will miss opportunities to demonstrate God's love and see those who mistreat us discover God's love.

The Results of Christ's Suffering

16. Read 1 Peter 2:24. What great truth of salvation is conveyed in this verse?

Christ's suffering accomplished the great result of our salvation! The great truth of the substitutionary death of Christ is that in "his own self" He bore our sins. He did not die for His own sins, for He had none. He died to take the punishment for the sins of all the people of the world (1 Timothy 2:6). He took our place (2 Corinthians 5:21).

Christ bore our sins in His body on the cross at Calvary. He gave His life by horrendous crucifixion "that we, being dead to sins, should live unto righteousness." When we accepted the gift of eternal life, we became dead to sins (Romans 6:7–13). This does not mean that we do not sin anymore. It does mean that we do not have to obey the demands of the flesh and of Satan anymore. We are freed from the power of sin so that we now can "live unto righteousness." Before our salvation we could not live a righteous life. In the power of the Savior, we can.

What was healed by Christ's stripes (v. 24)? Some think this refers to physical healing. They teach that this verse forms the basis for physical healing ministries. They also come to the conclusion that anyone who is sick must be living in some kind of sin because Christ died to heal us physically. Obviously this interpretation of the phrase leads to discouraged believers who can't figure out what sin God wants them to confess before He will heal them.

The healing in verse 24 is a spiritual healing, not a physical one. Though all believers will one day be delivered from physical illness when their bodies are glorified, this verse is not promising that condition to people before that day.

17. Read 1 Peter 2:25. To what ministries of the Lord did Peter refer when he called Him the Shepherd and Bishop of our souls?

Peter used a common metaphor when he referred to people as sheep (v. 25). Like sheep, we all were lost and astray from our Shepherd, the Lord. In the words "sheep going astray" and "now returned unto the Shepherd," Peter described the past and present of each child of God. Jesus' death on the cross became the way to the Shepherd.

"Shepherd" conveys the loving attention of the One Who feeds, protects, and leads the flock. "Bishop" describes the Shepherd's ministry in the oversight of those who were once wanderers but are now united as a flock.

18. What are the results of Christ's suffering?

Our Savior is the great example of One Who suffered unjustly yet triumphed in His suffering. His example won for us our great salvation and sets the standard for our response to our own suffering.

Making It Personal

19. How have you done at responding to suffering?

20. Which of Christ's responses to suffering do you need to incorporate into your life?

21. Memorize 1 Peter 2:21.

Marriage Matters

*Both husbands and wives have responsibilities
in the marriage relationship.*

1 Peter 3:1–7

"Ye wives, be in subjection to your own husbands. . . . Likewise, ye husbands, dwell with them according to knowledge, giving honour unto the wife, as unto the weaker vessel" (1 Peter 3:1a, 7a).

When is a marriage in trouble? Here are at least ten symptoms of a troubled marriage: (1) leaving little jobs undone, because of not feeling appreciated; (2) flirting with others; (3) enlisting family members in the couple's disputes; (4) not talking to each other because of having little in common; (5) repeatedly arguing over the same subject; (6) failing to please the other spouse—about anything; (7) no longer sharing information with the other spouse; (8) declining physical affection and intimacy; (9) declining hygiene or appearance; (10) constantly looking for distractions from one another.

It's not hard to imagine how these problems can snowball to affect relationships with others in and outside the family.

Getting Started

1. What are some of the people, like their children, that a married couple's relationship will affect?

2. How did your parents' marriage relationship affect you?

3. What did you learn about marriage from watching your parents?

The husband-wife relationship impacts a whole host of people. Peter addressed that relationship as an opportunity for husbands and wives to demonstrate Christ's type of submission.

Searching the Scriptures

The Christian Wife

4. Read 1 Peter 3:1. What is the significance of "likewise" in 3:1? To what previous passage/example does it refer?

Scripture teaches that the Christian wife should recognize the role of headship given to her husband: "Be in subjection to your own husbands" (v. 1).

5. What does "subjection" mean?

6. Does it imply inferiority? Explain.

The relationship between God the Father and God the Son helps us understand the relationship between a husband and wife. The Bible clearly teaches that God the Father and God the Son are absolutely equal in all their characteristics and abilities. However, the Son's role during His life on earth definitely placed Him in submission to the Father. Likewise, God created men and women equal in personal worth and standing before Him. Also, in a marriage, He has established a head-submission relationship. This plan is God's design, not a male scheme, although some men have abused their role (Genesis 3:16; 1 Timothy 2:11–14).

The head-submission principle is illustrated by women of the Old Testament. Peter used Sarah's relationship to Abraham as a specific example of a submissive wife.

Some Christian wives in Peter's day faced the challenge that their husbands knew the gospel message but had so far refused to accept it. Peter encouraged these wives by saying their husbands could be won to Christ by the wives' holy living.

7. What are some problems that might arise for a wife of an unbelieving husband?

8. How might an unsaved husband be won to Christ without a word from his wife?

The wives should not pressure their husbands for decisions by incessantly bringing up the subject of their spiritual condition. "Without the word" means that without the wife's further speaking to the issue, the husband could be won to Christ through the testimony of his wife's godly behavior.

Unbelievers continually watch believers, often to criticize, but also to note the genuineness of their profession. This is especially true in the close circles of the family and in the even more intimate relationship of a husband and wife. In no situation is there a greater need for a chaste, pure manner of life, motivated by fear or reverence for God and a sincere desire to please Jesus Christ.

Peter clarified the concept of subjection by appealing to the example of Sarah and other unnamed women of the Bible.

9. Read 1 Peter 3:5. What one word in this verse characterizes the relationship the Old Testament women had with God?

10. Why was their trusting relationship with God so foundational to their submission to their husbands?

We are told that Sarah obeyed her husband and called him "lord" (Genesis 18:12). This may not seem too significant, but to Peter's readers the term was a testimony of Sarah's submission to Abraham. The word "lord" shows respect, leadership, and recognition of the one responsible for the operation. Wives who evidence this kind of subjection toward their husbands join the ranks of Sarah as her daughters, as long as they do well and are not overcome with anxieties and fears.

Peter then changed began talking about adornment for women. He rejected three particular forms of adornment as improper: arranging hair, putting on gold jewelry, and wearing fine clothes.

11. What was Peter saying about outward adorning? Was he trying to keep believing women from doing anything to make themselves more attractive?

Obviously Peter did not intend to rule out all hairdressing and gold jewelry any more than he intended to forbid all clothing. He was communicating a basic Christian value that genuine beauty comes from within a person rather than from the physical exterior. Perhaps these Christian wives, anxious to please their unconverted husbands, were depending more on fashions than on the beauty of inner character developed by the Lord Jesus Christ. Peter raised their sights to higher standards.

12. Read 1 Peter 3:4. What does God desire to see in women?

"The hidden man of the heart" refers to the inner character that is recognized and highly valued by God because it has spiritual and eternal value. A Christian woman's best adornment is her Christ-centered personality as the Holy Spirit displays His graces in and through her life. The graces Peter mentioned are a meek and quiet spirit (v. 4) and a spirit of proper subjection (v. 5).

A wife who has a meek and quiet spirit will not nag, sabotage, or scream angry abuse. She will refrain from embarrassing or degrading her husband (Proverbs 21:9).

13. Name a woman with an obvious meek and quiet spirit.

14. How would you characterize that woman's relationships?

A spirit of quiet submission does not mean that a wife has no voice. She should be free to discuss matters with her husband, expressing her views and the reasons behind them. But when she and her husband do not reach the same conclusion and a decision must be made, she will allow him to make the decision and bear his responsibility for it before God.

The Christian Husband

Peter's (and God's) admonition for husbands to "dwell with them [their wives] according to knowledge" requires the husband to recognize facts about his wife as he lives with her. He must seek to understand her temperament, her personality, her needs, her strengths, and her weaknesses. The husband should act toward her in light of these. He must not treat her in the same way he thinks about himself. God made her different, and the husband needs to recognize, to accept, and to appreciate that truth.

15. Read 1 Peter 3:7. How can a husband learn about his wife?

To honor his wife means that the husband is to make her feel like she is someone very special, because indeed she is! She is God's gift. His life is bound together with hers in a covenant before God. He is to respect and elevate her. She should be honored because she is the "weaker vessel," which probably refers to the fact that God made women generally weaker physically than men.

16. What can a husband do to honor his wife?

17. How frequent should these demonstrations of honor be?

A husband should recognize that there exists between him and his wife a common spiritual bond, as well as emotional and physical ties. A Christian husband and wife are "heirs together of the grace of life" (v. 7).

This is total equality in their privilege of relationship with God. Beyond the natural pleasure of each other's companionship as Christians, they should enjoy mutual spiritual fellowship with the Lord and in His Word. In the blessings of eternal life, a wife is not weaker or inferior or ranked beneath her husband. The two are joint heirs, sharing in common the blessings of Christ.

Failure on the husband's part to display an understanding of his wife, to omit the special protection and tenderness due the weaker vessel, will hinder or interrupt prayer life. These failures displease God so greatly that He will turn a deaf ear toward the offender.

18. What does the consequence of a husband's failure to honor his wife tell you about how important the command is?

All husbands need to pay attention to the instruction to honor their wives and then actively seek to do so. A husband cannot use the excuse that he doesn't understand his wife. God holds him responsible to learn about her and then act accordingly.

Marriage roles are important to God. When a husband and wife fail in their responsibilities to each other, they will cause far-reaching consequences. Yet, those couples who embrace their roles will realize tremendous blessings.

19. What are some consequences of a couple's failure to carrying out their God-given roles?

20. What are some blessings of a couple's carrying out their God-given roles?

Though submission is a word often associated with the role of the wife, both the husband and wife must submit to God by carrying out the roles He has given to them.

Making It Personal

21. How will behaving properly as a husband or wife help you handle your trials?

22. When have you found that an unsettled marriage made the trials in your life so much more difficult to bear?

23. If you are a woman, what are some ways you can begin to show a meek and quiet spirit?

24. If you are a husband what are some ways in which you could honor your wife more?

25. Memorize 1 Peter 3:1a and 7a.

Building Lasting Relationships

God gives us instructions on building lasting relationships.

1 Peter 3:8–12

"Finally, be ye all of one mind, having compassion one of another, love as brethren, be pitiful, be courteous" (1 Peter 3:8).

In the late 1890s, Sir Thomas Bouch designed a bridge over the Firth of Tay. Tragically, he under-designed the structure and used cast iron. The weakened bridge swayed and collapsed one night, killing seventy-five passengers and crew. The people of Scotland became understandably leery about bridges.

When engineers proposed bridging the Firth of Forth, the Scottish public demanded near perfection. The result was the first bridge built primarily of steel. This railway bridge has a cantilever design, is 8,276 feet long (the longest bridge for many years), and has a center span of 350 feet. It required 54,000 tons of steel; 194,000 cubic yards of granite, stone, and concrete; 21,000 tons of cement; and almost seven million rivets. And it cost a whopping $15 million. In human expense, building the bridge cost 98 men their lives and injured more than 450. The Forth Railway Bridge is one of the strongest, and most expensive, in the world.

Getting Started

1. Would you trust a bridge that you had engineered and constructed? Why or why not?

2. Why must bridges be constructed so carefully?

3. How is building a bridge like building a relationship?

Peter gave instructions to his readers on how to build lasting relationships. Those instructions are the focus of this lesson.

Searching the Scriptures

Be of One Mind

4. Read 1 Peter 3:8a. What do you think describes two people who are of the same mind?

Believers share a common salvation, one Savior and Lord; the same source of truth, the Word of God; and the same Teacher, the Holy Spirit. They have a common pursuit in life, a common hope, and a common task to fulfill. Because of all they share, believers should be "of one mind." This does not demand unity in every minute detail, but we believers will express oneness of mind in our united focus on pleasing

God and in our united understanding of the major doctrines and practices of His Word.

5. Read Philippians 2:3–8. What do these verses tell you about what it means to have one mind?

6. Who has the model mind for all believers?

7. What characterizes His mind?

8. Name three people with whom you believe you share "one mind."

Be Compassionate, Loving, and Tenderhearted

"Having compassion" in verse 8 means to feel deeply with fellow Christians—with both their sorrows and their joys. "Sympathetic" is a good word to describe this relationship-building characteristic. Paul echoed this sentiment in Romans 12:15, when he called on believers to weep with those who weep and rejoice with those who rejoice. Notice Paul didn't say to criticize with those who criticize. A critical spirit toward the needy is sometimes a way of excusing ourselves from helping them; we dismiss the need from our minds by pointing out a flaw in the person.

9. How do you respond when you hear a fellow believer has a need? Do you think of how you can help him, or do you think of what excuse you might give to avoid helping him?

10. How will excusing ourselves from helping fellow believers affect our relationships with them?

Being sympathetic comes more easily for some people than it does for others, but all believers have a responsibility to show sympathy. When we do, our relationships will grow stronger.

11. When have you experienced an overwhelming show of sympathy from a person or group of believers?

12. How did their sympathetic actions affect your relationships with those people?

"Love as brethren" in verse 8 expresses the fondness and personal concern that we should manifest to fellow believers because we belong to the same family.

When a person is hurt or in danger, his family members will respond with urgency and great concern. Believers ought to respond to each other with the same urgency and concern. Our familial bond from being part of the Body of Christ should cause us to love each other as deeply as we love our blood relatives.

"Be pitiful" is a reminder to be tenderhearted, rather than calloused in our feelings toward others. We run the risk of becoming insensitive if we witness suffering and do not move to action.

13. What might cause believers to become calloused toward others?

Being compassionate, loving, and tenderhearted toward one another will go a long way toward developing lasting relationships. But to be all these things, we first need to be humble.

To be "courteous" (v. 8) is to be humble-minded. A humble person neither tears himself down nor beats himself up as if he is worthless. True humility is an honest evaluation of oneself. Romans 12:3 tells believers to think soberly, or honestly, about themselves and about the spiritual gifts God has given to them.

Humility is a special grace, a garment that is attractively suitable to Christ's disciples who follow in His steps (Colossians 3:12). It is also at the hub of what it takes to draw believers together into strong, lasting relationships.

14. When have you desired to build a friendship with someone who is obviously proud and stuck on himself?

15. Why wouldn't you want to build such a friendship?

Humility is what tells our selfish flesh to take a backseat as we reach out to help others. It moves us to act when we don't always feel like it, because we don't see ourselves as too important to spend time meeting people's needs.

Use Kind Words

Believers who are mistreated should not retaliate in kind, "not rendering evil for evil" (v. 9). Those who exhibit road rage violate this directive. When someone cuts a person off or nearly hits another's car, the natural tendency is to react with instant rage and a vengeful line of curses.

16. What are some other situations in which you have witnessed people retaliating without much thought?

Believers should not speak evil or be guilty of railing (v. 9), of scolding or reprimanding someone in an outburst of anger (Romans 12:17). First Thessalonians 5:15 leaves no room for such actions. It says we believers are to "ever," or always, follow what is good. Furthermore, believers should keep their tongues from evil and speak no guile or deceit (v. 10).

17. How do outbursts of anger, evil speaking, and deception affect relationships?

18. Read 1 Peter 3:11. Believers must also avoid ("eschew") evil. Why is avoiding evil important in building lasting relationships with other believers?

All of these are sins related to talking, which, if allowed to continue unchecked and unconfessed, stir up strife. Rather than speaking carelessly or selfishly, we believers must pursue peace and speak a blessing (vv. 9, 11). A believer who is able to pursue peace with someone who has hurt him with his words is a testimony to the power of God in his life. Pursuing peace and speaking blessings takes strength that only God's grace can provide.

Reasons for the Instructions

Peter gave four reasons for these instructions on building relationships.

First, they show us the way of Christ (v. 9). We believers are called to follow Christ, and at no time did the Lord render evil for evil (v. 9). Jesus is our supreme example for relationships and all of life. Peter's instructions shed further light on the way of Christ.

Second, these instructions lead to reward (v. 9). Peter said we will "inherit a blessing." The full enjoyment of our Christian life can be ours only when we express toward others the same patience and forgiveness that God has expressed toward us (Ephesians 4:32). The ultimate reward for treating others as we ought will come in eternity, when no measure of patience and forgiving spirit will be left unnoticed by Jesus Christ.

19. What kind deed have you done for someone lately that Christ will make sure does not go unrecognized?

Third, these instructions on relationship-building bring meaning to life (v. 10). The Christian who learns such godly manners will enjoy a satisfying, meaningful life. This is not always a long life, but it is one that will be free of bitterness and frustration.

Believers who harbor grudges about being wronged—and who stew about how they wish everyone else would change in order to please them—end up wasting their lives and often their health. Bitterness is an attempt to hurt others that backfires. Life becomes drudgery and full of sadness when we choose not to pursue peace and bless others.

Fourth, these relationship-building instructions prepare us to give an answer to God (v. 12). Both Christians and non-Christians must answer to the Lord. Furthermore, He is aware of our thorns. Such thorns may actually be instruments loaded with grace for our enrichment (2 Corinthians 12:9, 10). "For the eyes of the Lord are over the righteous" means He looks favorably on His children and has their best interests at heart. We can trust Him and commit the pain caused by evildoers to His righteous judgment.

Striving to follow Peter's instructions about building godly, lasting relationships will never be something we regret. In fact, it will be something we rejoice about for all of eternity if we get busy and do it now in the Lord's gracious strength.

Making It Personal

20. What trials in your life could you have avoided if you had lived out the instructions of 1 Peter 3:8–12?

21. How can you use that regret to spur yourself on to obedience from this point forward?

22. What steps do you need to take toward building strong, godly, lasting relationships?

23. From whom do you need ask forgiveness for the way you have treated them?

24. Are you holding grudges that you need to surrender to the Lord?

25. Are you neglecting the needs of people around you? Have you grown cold and calloused toward others?

26. Memorize 1 Peter 3:8.

Encouragement in Trials

God wants us to see trials as opportunities.

1 Peter 3:13–22

"But sanctify the Lord God in your hearts: and be ready always to give an answer to every man that asketh you a reason of the hope that is in you with meekness and fear" (1 Peter 3:15).

Strong-willed and independent, highly intelligent and determined—that was Helen Roseveare, a British doctor who served in the Congo from 1953 to 1973. In addition to practicing medicine, Helen built a 100-bed hospital and maternity complex, trained a hundred medical assistants, and established almost 50 rural clinics. Her story is told in the book *Though Lions Roar* and in the film *Mama Luka Comes Home*. She also wrote two books of her own: *Give Me This Mountain* (1966) and *He Gave Us a Valley* (1976).

Helen stayed in the Congo through the dangerous, unstable '60s. Many missionaries left the Congo at that time. But Helen believed the needs were great and God wanted her to remain. She adopted her mission's motto as her own: "If Christ be God and died for me, then no sacrifice can be too great for me to make for him." So she stayed.

In spite of being in the Congo to serve God—of doing the right thing—Helen suffered horribly. In 1964, rebel forces broke into her bungalow, beat and raped her, and took her prisoner for five months. They poured out on Helen their hatred of white men for the white men's injustices, cruelties, and more.

After her release, Helen returned to England. Two years later she was back in the Congo to help establish a new medical school and hospital. She left the Congo for the last time in 1973.

Getting Started

1. What are some examples of suffering for doing wrong?

2. What are some other examples of suffering for doing right?

3. When have you suffered for doing right?

Do trials or the threat of persecution allow Christians the option of setting aside Biblical principles and behaving like everybody else in the interest of self-preservation? Peter addressed this question in the next section of his letter.

Searching the Scriptures

Do What Is Good

4. Read 1 Peter 3:13. What point does the rhetorical question in this verse make?

Verse 13 serves as a bridge between the idea of minimizing suffering by being good (vv. 8–12) to the fact that sometimes people who do good suffer (vv. 14ff).

5. Do you expect to suffer for doing good? Explain.

Peter knew it was entirely possible for his readers to experience great suffering; some already had. However, it was important that they be able to discern whether their suffering was a matter of persecution for their godly testimony (John 15:18–21) or justly deserved punishment as a consequence for wrong behavior. Believers should not be doing evil things that would trigger punishment.

The human heart can be so perverse that occasionally people, irritated by the godliness of others, rise up against those doing right, and falsely accuse or persecute them.

Be Happy

6. Read 1 Peter 3:14. As what should we regard ourselves if we find we are being persecuted for doing right?

When we are persecuted, we are not to be paralyzed with fear (as the persecutors desire) and so lose our confidence. Neither are we to think and act as though "the eyes of the Lord" are no longer over the righteous (v. 12).

7. Read 1 Peter 3:17. What plain statement did Peter make in this verse?

Suffering is suffering, but suffering for the sake of obeying the Lord brings God's blessings now and in eternity. The blessings make the suffering valuable to the believer.

Additionally, in spite of suffering, we believers have hope. We may be called on to "give an answer," to explain the hope that is in us at any moment.

Sanctify Christ

8. Read 1 Peter 3:15. How might a believer make his "hope" evident while he is being persecuted?

As Christians, we must know the Word of God and be able to support what we profess. The word "answer" in verse 15 was a term used in the courts. It implies the giving of a verbal defense against some charge. It means that Christians should always stand ready to defend their beliefs and behavior on the basis of God's Word.

9. Why should we give the reason for our hope in a spirit of "meekness" (v. 15)?

Arrogance has no place in our defense for we are children of God, not by merit or greater discernment, but only by His sovereign act and mercy (1 Peter 1:2, 3). Our testimony of the unique hope that is ours should be gentle and respectful, "with meekness and fear."

Good Conscience

10. Read 1 Peter 3:16. What did Peter say is important for the persecuted believer to do as he verbally testifies of the hope in him?

Verse 16 is similar to 1 Peter 2:12. In addition to having a ready answer (v. 15), we Christians must also have a good conscience. Our manner of living must support our verbal witness.

Greatest Example

As in an earlier passage (2:21–23), Peter thought of the suffering of
Christ when he wrote about the suffering of believers. Christ suffered,
and so it is not strange that His people would suffer too. But the Savior
handled the suffering successfully, so He offers great hope and comfort
to suffering saints.

11. Read 1 Peter 3:18. What do we know about Christ by calling
Him "just"?

Christ, the pure and innocent One, was charged with the sins and
guilt of the guilty ones. He became the sinners' substitute.

Christ's sacrifice is set apart from all the Old Testament sacrifices,
for His sacrifice did not have to be repeated. His one death served as
the adequate payment for all sins. Therefore God, accepting His Son's
sacrifice, can be both just (demanding that sin be punished) and at the
same time can grant forgiveness to sinners.

Christ's suffering made it possible for Him to extend one hand to
sinners and another hand to a holy Father, and bring the two together
at the cross. The barrier between God and man was removed because
the full penalty for God's broken law was paid. Now sinners who receive the Son may come into the Holy of Holies, into God's very presence.

12. How do you think the persecuted believers responded when
they were reminded of the suffering Jesus endured on their behalf (v.
18, cf. 2:21)?

How was this great redemptive work made possible? Verse 18 offers an explanation: "Being put to death in the flesh, but quickened by the Spirit." Here Peter testified to the reality of Christ's physical death, which was essential if He were to fulfill all the Old Testament sacrifices of lambs, bullocks, goats and turtledoves. "Without shedding of blood is no remission [of sin]" (Hebrews 9:22).

But death was not the end of the story. For Christ to remain dead would have indicated that sin's penalty was not fully paid. "Quickened by the Spirit" could also read "quickened [made alive] in the spirit," speaking not of the Holy Spirit but of Jesus Christ's human spirit. It is true that the Holy Spirit raised up Christ's body after three days (Romans 8:11), but Peter here may have been explaining that Jesus' human spirit, which He had commended to His Father on the cross, continued to live while His body was in the tomb and then resided in His resurrection body.

The Announcement

In His quickened human spirit Christ engaged in a necessary ministry described in verses 19–21. Few if any commentators agree on this difficult passage. Here is one explanation:

In His resurrected body, into which His spirit had returned, Christ literally went into the prison house of condemned spirits and there announced these things: (1) God had dealt justly with sin by giving His sinless Son to die for the sins of men; (2) the wicked designs of the enemy had been thwarted; (3) their eternal punishment was now made sure because Christ held the keys of death and Hades in His resurrected hands. This was not an announcement of the gospel or of a second chance to be saved—it was a proclamation of victory.

Possibly Peter used the illustration of Noah's time because of his own interest in the Flood (2 Peter 2:5; 3:6) and also because Noah suffered much as a preacher of righteousness in an age that completely rejected his testimony.

13. How does the example of Noah's suffering for 120 years as he labored to build the ark in a hostile environment help you put any suffering you experience for God into perspective?

Verse 20, then, speaks of a special time when God in great patience waited expectantly for some response during the 120 years of preparation for the Food. No one beyond Noah's family responded. That family was saved through the flood that destroyed the disobedient. The God-provided ark saved them as that ark was raised above the judgment by the very waters of judgment.

Our Salvation

14. Read 1 Peter 3:21. What might someone conclude about baptism from reading this verse without studying it?

Some say verse 21 teaches that baptism is needed for salvation. Three particular points indicate that this passage cannot teach that baptism saves a person.

First, Noah and his family were not saved "by" water. A better translation for the end of verse 20 is "through the water" (the preposition bears both meanings). It was the ark, which was God's provision for them, that saved them. And in a greater sense, it was their faith in God and in His provision that saved them. The water was a means of death to those who did not believe.

Furthermore, verse 21 states specifically that baptism does not save us. Salvation does not come by "the putting away of the filth of the flesh, but the answer of a good conscience toward God," and that good conscience can come only by trusting Christ as Savior.

Finally, if verse 21 taught that baptism saves us, it would contradict other clear Scriptures which declare that faith in Christ alone is needed for salvation (Acts 16:31; Ephesians 2:8, 9). Therefore, this text cannot mean that baptism is needed for salvation. What, then, does it mean?

Peter said in verse 20 that the ark brought eight people safely through the water. He then said that baptism is a "figure" which corresponds to that. What does baptism figure? It figures, or shows, a person's belief in Christ as Savior. Belief in Christ's work on his behalf is what saves a person. As the ark brought the eight people safely through the flood, so our Ark, the Lord Jesus Christ, safely brings us through, and baptism shows this in a figurative way. The act of baptism is a visible expression of our faith in Christ's death, burial, and resurrection. It only shows what has already happened in our lives. It "figures" or "corresponds" to our salvation. Peter concluded this explanation by saying that the whole plan of redemption is made possible by the capstone of all Christ's works—His resurrection.

After His resurrection, Christ ascended to Heaven (Acts 1:9). He is now enthroned at God's right hand with all heavenly beings and authorities under His dominion, and He is waiting until God establishes His rule over all the earth.

15. Read Hebrews 12:2. What does this verse say about how Jesus feels now about the suffering He endured as the perfect Son of God?

Making It Personal

Christ is the ultimate example of suffering for doing good.

16. How might you "testify of Christ" when you respond Biblically to suffering?

17. How else might you testify of Christ?

One of the commands from the text is to be ready to give every man an answer for the hope that lies in us (v. 15). This command is given in the context discussing trials. We need to be ready to give anyone an answer who asks us about how we are facing our trials with hope.

18. What are some statements or questions people may make to us that should evoke a Christian response?

19. What are some Christian responses we could make?

20. Memorize 1 Peter 3:15.

Lesson 11

Eternal Values

Believers should live in light of eternity since our life on earth is so short.

1 Peter 4:1–11

"But the end of all things is at hand: be ye therefore sober, and watch unto prayer" (1 Peter 4:7).

W hat would you do for a living if you grew up partly in Washington, D.C., and partly in various foreign capitals? Or if you graduated Wellesley College with a degree in English? You might become a journalist or even a film critic, which is what Judith Perlman Martin did. Or you might make a slight switch to writing an advice column—also what Judith Martin did. You might know Mrs. Martin as Miss Manners. Her answers to etiquette questions are printed in 200 newspapers worldwide. "Miss Manners" writes with an admonishing tone and sarcasm, a broad knowledge of history and customs, and insight into applying customs to situations today. In short, Judith Martin is an authority on etiquette.

Etiquette is the conduct required by good breeding or prescribed by authority to be observed in social or official life. In 1 Peter 4, Peter laid out some of what we could call "Christian etiquette for the end times."

Getting Started

1. When have you appreciated another believer's conduct during suffering?

2. When has anyone ever commented on your "Christian etiquette," or conduct, during suffering?

3. Do you agree or disagree that the end times should affect your conduct? Explain.

Searching the Scriptures

The opening statement of chapter 4 turns our attention back to 1 Peter 3:18. Christ's suffering was for sins—not His sins but ours. Not only did Christ endure pain as we know pain, but He experienced the agonizing death of crucifixion. He did all of this in a voluntary expression of love and mercy, "the just for the unjust."

Arm Yourselves

4. Read 1 Peter 4:1. What does the phrase "arm yourselves" convey about the difficulty of remaining godly in the face of suffering?

Believers should arm themselves with a certain attitude or mindset, which serves as their equipment for war. This mindset is "the same mind" as Christ had toward suffering. When He suffered, He did not threaten His persecutors, but committed Himself to the Father who judges righteously (2:23).

5. How can a believer "arm" himself with Christ's mindset?

6. What makes the gospel message so effective during persecution, a time when trusting Christ most likely means physical suffering?

Living to the Will of God

Each person must choose between two opposing standards as a pattern for personal moral conduct—the "lusts of men" or "the will of God." God calls believers to choose the path of living for the will of God and to renounce the lusts of men.

7. Why does persecution bring a believer's choice between living for self and living for God to a point of definite decision?

The life of a person who becomes a Christian can be divided into two portions: the "time past," prior to his conversion, and "the rest of his time in the flesh," after his conversion. By his manner of living the Christian should give evidence that his life prior to his salvation is a closed chapter. In that time past, he "wrought," or worked out, the "will of the Gentiles," which was basically after the flesh and manifested itself in such conduct as spoken of in 1 Peter 2:1 and 11 and 4:3.

8. Read 1 Peter 4:3. If you were saved later in life, what changed most dramatically about your life after your salvation?

9. How did your unsaved friends respond?

Breaking the Bondage

Non-Christians can be amazed when one of their number turns from old attitudes and conduct to faith in Jesus Christ and begins to act contrary to the normal demands of the flesh. They themselves are willing prisoners of the lusts of the flesh, so they cannot understand why these one-time friends "run not with them" (v. 4). What they cannot grasp is that God imparts to His children a new power (Romans 8:2) that breaks the bondage of the flesh. Christians possess a new nature and have escaped the corruption that is in the world through lusts (2 Peter 1:3, 4).

Many new Christians have tasted the bitter pill Peter called "speaking evil of you" in verse 4. At first, non-Christian friends express surprise at the new Christian's changed patterns of life. Some, of course, state that it won't last because it is so contrary to what they feel are the pleasures of life. But as the new Christian refuses invitations to certain behaviors and demonstrates new spiritual appetites, the unsaved friends of his previous life begin quite unjustly to accuse and slander him. Believers faced such treatment even in Peter's day.

10. Have you ever been criticized for refusing to "run" with the unsaved? What were the circumstances?

11. Read 1 Peter 4:5. What sobering truth about those who slander believers did Peter point out in this verse?

Peter identified the slanderers as those "who shall give account." They will be held accountable by God for their words. The One Who will judge is ready. His perfect knowledge provides all the facts, and His perfect justice balances His perfect love so that His judgment will be neither too soft nor too harsh. "The quick and the dead" plainly teaches that when God's judgment comes, it will be equally applicable and fair for both those then living and those who have died. (See 2 Timothy 4:1 and Acts 10:42.)

12. When you consider the judgment of slanderers, for whom do you feel sorrier, the slanderers or the believers they are slandering?

Justified

In verse 6, "the gospel preached also to them that are dead" refers to the proclamation of the gospel to those who were alive prior to Peter's writing but had died by the time he wrote. Having become Christians, they also became the objects of unjust persecution and were martyred for their faith.

"That they might be judged according to men in the flesh" is a difficult statement to understand, but it seems to mean that those who heard and believed were judged as guilty by their persecutors, while living (in the flesh), and were put to death. At the same time they were given life by God. Since God, the righteous Judge, shall judge the living and the dead, how much better it is to place our faith in Christ and thereby have His judgment against our sin satisfied while we are still living here. Those who had heard and believed the gospel of salvation stood declared justified before God, whereas the persecutors of Christians would still face their judgment.

Even though those martyred Christians are dead in body, they remain very much alive in the spirit and are enjoying spiritual life and fellowship with God—something their living detractors would never know unless they repented of their sin and received Christ.

13. Read 1 Peter 4:7. How have you allowed the any-moment return of Christ to affect how seriously you take living for Him?

Over nineteen hundred years have passed since Peter wrote "the end of all things is at hand" (v. 7), and still human history continues to move on. This does not discredit Peter's statement, for in the calendar of eternity, nineteen centuries is less than a speck. The Lord's coming remains imminent (possible at any moment), and the believer must live in light of it.

Be Sober and Pray

To be "sober" means to be of a sound mind in view of the fact that the end of all things is at hand, to keep a mental outlook that views life from God's perspective. The sober person will not be carried away by enthusiasm for some cause or point of view or movement that is not of God (cf. 2 Corinthians 11:3; Colossians 2:8).

14. What makes adopting a mindset of living for today and the matters of this world so easy?

Christians who are sober-minded recognize the value of watching "unto prayer" as events unfold prior to Christ's return. "Watch" means to keep oneself alert, calm, and "unbefuddled," for prayer demands our best diligence and energies. Christians who allow their mind to be restless, disturbed, and undisciplined will have a difficult time watching in prayer.

15. How can prayer help you keep your sights on eternity?

Love and Hospitality

While a believer's inner mind and personal prayer life need to be in order, living the Christian life impacts relationships with others. Verse 8 challenges us to have fervent charity, or love, toward fellow believers, a love that stretches our powers to their full extent. Love is the foundational characteristic of God's gracious working in us (1 Corinthians 13:13) and is the capstone of all the other graces (Colossians 3:14).

This love is to be demonstrated between believers, for it catches the eye of the unconverted (John 13:35). Love has a definite and a needed ministry among believers; it covers a "multitude of sins." Christians are not perfect, and they can be irritating; but the grace of love majors on protecting our brothers and sisters rather than lifting the cover to publicize their weaknesses before the unsaved. This does not mean overlooking sin in a brother or sister, but it does mean dealing with the matter in ways that do not stimulate gossip.

16. Who is the focus of a gossiper's love?

17. Evaluate this statement: A gossiper cannot expose someone's sin without also exposing his own.

18. Read 1 Peter 4:9. Describe the blessings you have experienced from showing hospitality to fellow believers.

Peter also advocated that Christians practice hospitality without grudging or murmuring, to be friendly to strangers even if the burden was heavy. Restaurants and motor lodges were centuries away, so it was essential that believers open their homes to one another, especially since traveling Christians were often rejected by former friends who were yet unsaved. To some, the practice of hospitality meant hardship; but they were to avoid complaining. Rich rewards would be theirs as they practiced what Christ taught (Matthew 25:35–40; 2 Corinthians 9:7, 8; Hebrews 13:2).

Gifts for God's Glory

19. Read 1 Peter 4:10 and 11. What do you believe are your spiritual gifts?

20. How well are you putting them into practice?

In view of the end of all things, we each should exercise our special spiritual enabling granted to us by the Holy Spirit so that we may fulfill our appointed task in the Body of Christ and in the local church (1 Corinthians 12:4–7). The gift one receives is determined by a sovereign God, but the proper exercise of that gift is the individual's responsibility. Since no believer is without a gift, and since no believer has all the gifts, we must depend on one another for the fullest of fellowship and for the most complete ministry. God has raised up the local church to carry out the Great Commission. To this end He gave gifts of men and women to the church to enable them to fulfill their place.

In verse 11 Peter simply enlarged on the nature of the spiritual gift. He spoke of two classes of gifts—those related to the spoken word and those related to service ministries. Since ability—either with the mouth or with the hand—comes from God, all jealousy, pride, and boasting are excluded. God doesn't divide service into the sacred and the secular if it is a service rendered to Him. The purpose of the ministries is that God may be glorified through His Son Jesus Christ, to Whom we redeemed owe all that we are or will be.

Making It Personal

21. Name some things that could distract you from living in light of eternity.

22. How can you eliminate or minimize those distractions in your life?

23. What one specific change will you make in how you use your time?

24. Memorize 1 Peter 4:7.

Glorify God in Your Trials

God wants us to purpose to glorify Him in trials.

1 Peter 4:12–19

"Yet if any man suffer as a Christian, let him not be ashamed; but let him glorify God on this behalf" (1 Peter 4:16).

Lori likes to work with plastic canvas. For a while she was into making little rectangular plaques in two colors. She kept one in her favorite color, purple. If you were to look at the dark purple part, you would see an abstract design of dark and light purple. But if you concentrated on the light purple, you would see the words "Jesus Saves." It's all a matter of perspective.

Perspective—we all have it. We have it visually. It's how objects appear to our eyes in respect to their relative distance and positions—thus the difference between the abstract design and the spelled out sentiment in Lori's craft.

Cognitively we have perspective. It's our point of view, our choice of a context for the things we experience and believe. Psychologically we have it (although some have it more than others). It is wisdom or the capacity to view things in their true relations or relative importance.

Getting Started

1. When have you had differing visual perspectives on some object?

2. Describe a time when you had a different perspective after an event than you had before it.

3. When have you had a different point of view from your spouse or close friend?

Believers have differing perspectives on a wide range of subjects, but we should have the same perspective on suffering. First Peter 4:12–19 spells out several results of having a Biblical perspective on suffering.

Searching the Scriptures

Expect Suffering

4. Read 1 Peter 4:12. What did Peter tell the suffering believers not to think about their fiery trials?

5. When have you had a wrong perspective about your trials?

Apparently some suffering believers were thinking that something had gone astray with the divine plan. They reasoned that the godly shouldn't suffer, especially unjustly, at the hands of God's enemies. Was God ignorant of their plight or impotent to help or calloused to their tears? Not at all, said Peter, trials are not abnormal. In fact, they are part of the blueprint as God transforms redeemed sinners into the image of His Son (Romans 8:29). Trials sometimes serve as God's smelting furnace, where the impurities of self-love, self-pity, pride, bitterness, lack of concern for others, and sinful desires are removed by God's strong but loving hand. Other times God uses trials to open ministry opportunities and further His work.

We often use the word "happen" to mean that an event seemed to have no cause or purpose—it just happened.

6. When was the last time you said, "I can't believe this just happened!"?

From the divine viewpoint, nothing just "happens." Nero was on the throne as Peter wrote, but that was not just chance. The persecution at Jerusalem that scattered the believers everywhere didn't just happen. God keeps these things under His control (Romans 8:28) and is fully aware of what is going on.

Rejoice in Suffering

7. Read 1 Peter 4:13. What did Peter tell the believers to do in regard to their trials?

8. Have you ever followed that instruction in the midst of your trials?

The verb for "rejoice" is in the present tense and indicates that rejoicing is to characterize the believer. Rejoicing is a matter of both attitude and activity. The attitude produces the activity.

Peter's readers would have no cause to rejoice in trials that resulted from their own failures, but they could and should rejoice in the prospect of unjust suffering. If they were sharing in Christ's sufferings, they were assured that they would also share in His glory hereafter.

9. What would the believers experience as a result of sharing in God's glory (v. 13)?

Not all reproaches are cause for rejoicing. It is possible to suffer for attitudes, words, and conduct improper for a Christian. In such cases, the discomfort of suffering should stir the erring Christian to repentance.

Those who suffer reproach for the name of Christ are usually those who willingly bear His name, those who gladly identify themselves as followers of Jesus Christ. Such Christians are the ones who demonstrate His unique lordship in their lives.

To be reproached by people—scorned, discredited, disgraced—for being righteous should not be viewed as a tragic misfortune to be avoided at all cost. Such reproaches are not occasions for sackcloth and ashes or overemotional self-pity, but are opportunities for showing gladness. In reality the reproach of the world for our consistent testimony is an occasion for celebrating that we are permitted to join the ranks of such an elect people (Acts 5:40, 41).

Peter wrote, "For the spirit of glory and of God resteth upon you" (1 Peter 4:14). This refers to the Holy Spirit Himself. We could rephrase Peter's words to read: "For the Spirit of glory, even the Spirit of God is resting upon you." Here is a divine activity on behalf of the reproached believer, a sign that God is aware of his pressing need. The word "rest" is used in Matthew 11:28 and refers to giving aid to a person who is weary and burdened down so he can experience rest. Here the Lord is saying through Peter that the Holy Spirit not only dwells within the believer, but He gives the believer inner rest in spite of the reproaches.

10. How important has the ministry of the Holy Spirit been in your life as you experience trials?

Glorify God in Suffering

In the first part of verse 16, Peter reminded his readers that if they suffered for being Christians, they should not feel ashamed. Rather, they should glorify God. This brings a new dimension into the picture of suffering. Not only is the believer to bear up under the trials without complaining, but he is actually to glorify God in those trials.

11. How would you explain "glorify God" to a child?

To glorify God means to bring praise and adoration to Him. We do this by crediting God with our words and by living as God desires before others.

It is the responsibility of believers to respond to afflictions in a godly manner. Doing so demonstrates that the Spirit of Christ is resting on them and it glorifies the Father and His Son (Matthew 5:16).

Commit Your Soul to God

Peter encouraged the believers who were suffering "according to the will of God" (that is, for right doing and not for wrongdoing) to commit the keeping of their souls to Him (v. 19). This idea of committing has the thought of trusting the whole matter to God's care and not worrying. They could trust God to take care of the outcome because He is "a faithful Creator."

12. How does the description "faithful Creator" help in time of trial?

Mentioning that He is the Creator reminds us that God is all-powerful: He made everything by His word, and He controls all circumstances and situations. We know that in committing our souls to Him, we are putting ourselves in the hands of One Who can act powerfully on our behalf. Also, He is faithful; He would never leave us or forsake us (Hebrews 13:5). This was an ensured deposit!

Don't Suffer for Doing Wrong

Suffering should not come from doing wrong (4:15). Some of those receiving Peter's letter had been saved out of a wicked past. "Let none of you suffer." implies that some had suffered in their previous unconverted life because of ungodly conduct. The contrast between their present and past was to be so sharp that there could be no reproaches. Their former sinful activities were completely taboo to the new life (1 Corinthians 6:9–11; Ephesians 5:8). Some of them, like some of us, had been murderers, thieves, evildoers, busybodies. But God's marvelous grace brought them into the divine family and provided an eternal inheritance.

It is amazing what sins God lumps together, while we divide them into categories such as extremely evil, moderately evil, and tolerable. God puts covetousness on the same par as fornication (Colossians 3:5) or malice with blasphemy (v. 8). First Peter 4:15 condemns the busybody right along with the murderer. "Busybody" literally means "a supervisor of things not one's own." We might say, "a self-appointed overseer."

13. Why is putting sins into categories not a good idea?

Sometimes when Christians experience criticism, the critics are justified because those believers are busybodies, seeking to supervise things outside their control. God is not pleased with self-appointed overseers.

Suffer for Doing Right

In Peter's day, Christians were known as followers of Christ, Christ-like ones. How should a believer view the label "Christian"? "Let him not be ashamed," wrote Peter, even if identity with Christ leads to suffering (v. 16).

14. How would you label the level of persecution you experience as a believer: nonexistent, low, moderate, high, or extreme?

15. What are the reasons for your level of persecution?

The more we live for Christ, the more we should expect to suffer. A low level of suffering for Christ may be appropriate in a society that grants religious freedom. But we should be sure that a low level of suffering is not due to a lack of living for Christ and seeking to share the message of the gospel.

16. What are some actions you could take to increase the level of your persecution?

Judgment of the Believer

When Peter announced "the time is come that judgment must begin at the house of God" (1 Peter 4:17), he acknowledged that for his readers the fires of persecution had already begun and would shortly gather intensity.

The statement about the righteous scarcely being saved (v. 18) has nothing to do with the believer's eternal safety in salvation. The word "scarcely" bears the idea of "with difficulty." It is true that the righteous are saved with difficulty. Humanly speaking, it was not easy for God. It meant robbing Heaven for thirty-three years of His own Son. It meant the Father's anguish as the Son humbled Himself in the incarnation, was rejected by His own people, was vilified, mocked, abused, slapped, spat upon, forsaken, crucified, and made sin for us. It meant death and burial and finally the display of God's power in resurrection. It meant God's judgment on His special people, the Jews. The plan of salvation was brought to pass with difficulty.

Beyond that cost to the heart of God, we find Christians are like sheep having a tendency to stray. Often Christians must be disciplined by much sorrow. Such judgment begins with us (v. 17). Christians are often judged here and now, whereas nonbelievers have their judgment yet to come.

Judgment of the Unbeliever

First Peter 4:17 and 18 contain two questions about the unsaved: "What shall the end be of them that obey not the gospel of God?" and "Where shall the ungodly and the sinner appear?" Unbelievers face God's irrevocable law of sowing and reaping in this life. They may reap the penalty of wrongdoing from civil governments, but God is not in the business of purifying or judging the non-Christian in this life, as He does continuously for His child.

God has permitted—yes, even directed—suffering and judgment to come upon His own people for whom Christ died, so how much more serious will be His judgment upon those who persecute His children and reject His gospel.

17. How should God's coming judgment on the lost affect your desire to share the gospel message?

18. How should God's coming judgment on the lost affect your desire to live righteously before them?

The sin of those without Christ was twofold: first, their obstinate rejection of the truth, and second, their willful persecution of the believers without cause. Two categories are mentioned: (1) the sinners, those whose acts were contrary to the will of God, and (2) the ungodly, those who have omitted God from their lives and thoughts even though they may be regarded as upright in conduct. God's judgment for such people is held in restraint today so that grace and mercy may prevail and produce repentance (Romans 2:4). But every day's delay in obeying the gospel adds to the storehouse of God's wrath (Romans 2:5).

While suffering may come for doing right, we should never bring it upon ourselves by doing wrong. The unbeliever will suffer punishment.

Making It Personal

Handling trials does not mean we merely bear up under them passively. It means we glorify God actively and aggressively in our trials. This is going a step beyond what we normally think about in our times of trials to the point of living godly in our trials.

19. What are some ways to glorify God in times of trial?

20. Do you see how this will help us in handling our trials, which is the overall theme of 1 Peter?

21. In what three ways can you glorify God in one of your current trials?

22. Memorize 1 Peter 4:16.

All Your Care

God wants believers to cast their burdens on Him, for He cares for them.

1 Peter 5:1–14

"Humble yourselves therefore under the mighty hand of God, that he may exalt you in due time: Casting all your care upon him; for he careth for you" (1 Peter 5:6, 7).

In 1999, the 436th Security Forces Squadron began holding an annual Ruck March competition. Volunteer soldiers sign up to march in four-man teams for six miles, each wearing a thirty-pound rucksack. The march is a fundraiser to honor the veterans of the Korean War who fought in the Battle of the Chosin Reservoir.

One participant from the Air Force Mortuary Affairs Operations Center at Dover Air Force Base, Delaware, described his experience: "It was a perfect day, but it was definitely a challenge walking six miles with a thirty-pound load."

The soldiers who fought in the Battle of the Chosin Reservoir were not so fortunate. After seventeen days of fighting in sub-freezing temperatures and being outnumbered 10 to 1, they broke free of the Chinese lines and made a twenty-seven-mile retreat over mountainous terrain in frigid temperatures. They had to keep going even when they didn't think they could or didn't want to anymore. Upon reaching Hungnam, the veterans were evacuated as part of a large amphibious operation to rescue UN troops from northeastern Korea.

Getting Started

1. Have you ever gone backpacking?

2. How heavy was your backpack? What did the weight of your backpack do to your ability to navigate successfully the trail you were on?

3. How did you feel when you were finally able to take your pack off and move about without it?

Just as the veterans of Chosin Reservoir gladly lay down their burdens when they finally arrived in Hungnam, just as that Ruck March participant was glad to release his extra thirty-pound burden, and just as you gladly removed your rucksack or backpack, believers can take off their burdens—and leave them with Jesus. In 1 Peter 5, Peter gave instructions about leaving our burdens with the Lord.

Searching the Scriptures

Instructions to Pastors

4. Read 1 Peter 5:1. How did Peter identify himself?

Peter turned his attention to the pastors who were serving the various churches his letter would reach, and exhorted them about their pastoral ministries with the words "the elders which are among you I exhort."

The terms "pastor," "elder," and "bishop," or "overseer," are different titles for the same office and reveal different responsibilities of the man who holds that office (Acts 20:17, 28; Titus 1:5, 7).

Peter identified himself as an elder. By this he meant that he had a pastoral ministry to people (this letter was an example of it) and to other pastors. He further identified himself as a witness of the sufferings of Christ (at Christ's crucifixion) and a partaker of the glory that will come (the glory of Heaven).

5. Why do pastors need "pastoring"?

6. How can your church make sure your pastor gets "pastored"?

Feed the Flock

Peter wrote to pastors to "feed the flock of God which is among you" (1 Peter 5:2).

7. What would you say is implied with the command to "feed the flock"?

Just as parents provide nourishment for their children, so the pastor must provide spiritual nourishment from Scripture for the flock.

To feed the flock means to shepherd the flock. This involves leading, guiding, protecting, and sometimes rescuing strays. It means concern for the weak and helpless. The pastor is to act just as Christ, the Great Shepherd, would act if He were physically present.

8. How has your pastor fed you lately in a meaningful way?

Oversee the Flock

9. Read 1 Peter 5:2 and 3. Using three contrasting couplets, Peter explained how the pastor is to take the oversight of the church. Fill in the blanks to complete the couplets.

Not _____ but

_____

Not _____ but

_____

Not _____ but

_____

First, the pastor is to take the oversight of the flock God gives him. This responsibility involves administration and leadership plus an authority committed to him by the Scriptures and by the call of the church. This oversight must not be due to any sense of constraint ("I guess I have to do this"). Rather, it should be carried out willingly, gladly, and voluntarily.

10. How much success would you predict for a pastor who serves by constraint instead of willingly?

Second, the pastor should have a "ready mind," being eager to serve without being influenced by money. However, the pastor who serves well should receive generous compensation (1 Corinthians 9:11; 1 Timothy 5:18), but if money or financial gain becomes his purpose, his ministry will be in danger (1 Timothy 6:10; 1 Peter 5:2).

Third, the pastor should not act as a lord over God's heritage, but should be an example to his flock. God entrusts His "heritage," His people, to the pastor's care. The pastor is not to lead the flock by a high-handed, autocratic rule or dictatorship, but by his example of obedience to God.

Rewards for Faithfulness

11. Read 1 Peter 5:4. What is the reward for a faithful pastoral ministry?

Christ is coming, and every pastor will give an account for his ministry (Hebrews 13:7, 17). The crown that the faithful pastor receives will never fade away. It is called a crown of glory because it is a share in Christ's glory.

12. How are pastors like our counselors during trials?

Submit to Elders

"Elder" in verse 5 probably refers to those who were the older believers in the churches, not to the office of the elder or pastor. In matters that don't violate Christian conscience (as taught by the Word), those who are younger should always listen with respect to those who have lived longer, gained more experience, and earned—by their character and conduct—the right to be heard.

13. Would you say that younger believers respect older believers in general today? Explain.

The command to "all of you be subject one to another" in verse 5 echoes a principle developed in chapter 3. If all believers engaged in the practice of willing subjection in giving others honor, the example would make it much easier for the youth to do so to their elders. Christians should seize every opportunity to exercise self-denial for the blessing of others.

Be Humble

14. What does "be clothed with humility" mean (1 Peter 5:5)?

This phrase depicts the grace of not thinking too highly of our-selves (Romans 12:3). Humility does not dictate self-depreciation or a depressing view of one's self. Humility involves viewing ourselves re-alistically: God deserves credit for all that we are and have. This virtue should cover our being just as our clothing covers our bodies.

God knows how we act, and He treats us according (Psalm 138:6; Proverbs 3:34). Peter's warning that "God resisteth the proud" should teach us to walk humbly before Him and through the Holy Spirit daily die to pride and self-assertiveness. What believer wants the sovereign God resisting him because of an unbecoming, non-Christian attitude?

God bestows a positive favor to the humble. He "giveth grace" to those who are truly humble, following the pattern of Jesus Christ (Matthew 11:29).

15. When have you experienced God's grace after humbling your-self?

"Humble yourselves" means to permit ourselves to be humbled. This calls for active participation in the humbling process, not merely uninvolved resignation. A man with an affliction chooses a physician and willingly submits himself to this surgeon's knife, knowing the ben-efit of health to be gained. In a similar way the Christian, sensing the corrupting foe of pride, submits himself to God for corrective surgery. To display a spirit of humility is to be like Jesus Christ.

Cast Your Care on the Lord

Verse 7 is related to the context of submission and self-humbling. The unjust persecution that Peter's readers were experiencing was part of their humiliation. Their circumstances were conducive to worry, but they were to trust God's wisdom and goodness.

"Casting" means to "throw upon" and implies a conscious effort on our part—an act of the will in faith—to deposit with the Lord all our care. This includes all present and also all potential anxieties. We cannot prevent the troubles that cause anxiety, but we can rise above the anxieties caused by the troubles.

16. Why can you cast all your care on God (v. 7)?

"For he careth for you" assures us that God feels our pain and He has a design in mind, knowing exactly the degrees of heat in the furnace of adversity necessary to accomplish that design. Christians must build on the principle that God is too good to be unkind to us and too wise ever to make a mistake (Romans 8:31, 22).

17. How can you cast your burdens on the Lord?

18. What are some of the burdens believers should cast on Him?

Watch Out for Satan

19. Read 1 Peter 5:8. How does this verse describe the Devil?

To "be sober" means to be mentally alert. "Be vigilant" means to watch intently. The Christian has a mighty adversary who never rests, the Devil. Believers must always be alert and watchful lest this enemy creep up on their undefended, unwatched side.

Satan has the roar of a hungry animal, "seeking whom he may devour." His intent toward Peter's readers may have been to intensify the persecution, to weaken them, and cause them to deny their faith and thereby save their physical lives. In a broader sense, he would devour by prompting indulgence of the flesh and impurity of the mind, by corrupting their faith, by dulling their conscience, by cooling their fervor, and by silencing their testimony.

"Resist stedfast in the faith" is the Christian's strategy against the enemy of the soul. Such resistance does not mean to challenge Satan to duel, but to stand firm against him. Christians are incapable of fighting with the Devil, for Satan is of superior strength and intelligence plus vast experience. He has been in the ring with professionals, and we are rank amateurs. But we can stand firm before him with the believer's warfare equipment (Ephesians 6:13–18).

To be "stedfast" means to stand firmly and solidly, as a body of heavily armed soldiers would stand shoulder to shoulder against the enemy. This solid resistance is "in the faith," in the truth of Christ that has been given to us. We stand firmly on the whole counsel of God, for the Word of truth is the only sword effective against the father of lies. One incentive for taking this stand was the believers in other parts of the world who were going through similar afflictions.

20. How can you support your fellow believers better during trials?

Final Remarks

21. Read 1 Peter 5:10. Identify the two contrasting time phrases in verse 10. How would those phrases encourage Peter's readers?

Peter desired that God, the God of grace Who had called his readers to salvation and eternal glory through Christ, would perfect them (equip them; Ephesians 4:12), establish them (make them solid or steadfast), and strengthen them (impart to them power for performance). Peter said this would come after they had suffered, showing that God uses difficult time in believers' lives for their own good. Peter then praised the Lord (v. 11).

He then stated the purpose of his brief letter as "exhorting, and testifying," or encouraging and assuring his readers. They were not to feel that their faith was in something false just because they were suffering. Peter enclosed a greeting from the "elect" (believers) of Babylon and from Mark. He expressed his warm affection for them in the closing verse.

The final chapter of Peter's letter teaches us that suffering believers of every age group and every position can cast their cares on God. We all know that we should let go of them and trust Him to take our burdens in times of trial, but we often find it difficult to do what we know.

Making It Personal

22. What is your greatest burden right now? Write a prayer to the Lord, telling Him that you are giving that burden over to Him, that it is His, that you will no longer worry about it or try to find a way out of it in your own strength and wisdom.

23. What would you say is the most meaningful lesson you learned from this study on 1 Peter?

24. What encouraged you the most?

25. What challenged you the most?

26. Memorize 1 Peter 5:6 and 7.